Jonah

BIBLE STUDY

Adriel Sanchez *with*

Josh Maloney

C·C

Jonah: Bible Study

by Adriel Sanchez with Josh Maloney

© 2021 Core Christianity
13230 Evening Creek Drive
Suite 220–222
San Diego, CA 92128

Design and Creative Direction by Metaleap Creative
Cover Illustration by Peter Voth

Printed in the United States of America

First Printing July 2021

Contents

05   INTRODUCTION   Why This Study?

08   LESSON 1   Fleeing from God (1:1–3)

20   LESSON 2   The Sleeping Prophet (1:4–6)

30   LESSON 3   "What Is This You Have Done!" (1:7–10)

42   LESSON 4   The Sailors vs. The Sea (1:11–16)

52   LESSON 5   Jonah in the Fish (1:17–2:6)

62   LESSON 6   God Saves His Prophet (2:7–10)

74   LESSON 7   Again in God's Presence (3:1–5)

86   LESSON 8   God and the Great City (3:6–10)

98   LESSON 9   "Please Take My Life from Me" (4:1–4)

110   LESSON 10   The God of Compassion (4:5–11)

122   RESOURCES

Why *This* Study?

Introduction: Why This Study?

To begin, we would like to thank you—students, congregants, church leaders, elders, pastors, and churches—for supporting and using this Bible study. We hope it enriches your Christian life, challenges your heart, and builds up your faith to the glory of God.

Why Jonah?

Many people know the story of Jonah and the big fish, but few could say why it's in the Bible. And fewer still understand how Jonah's calling and message illuminate the redemption that would come through God's Son hundreds of years later. This Bible study will help us behold God's mercy and justice as it leads us into a deeper understanding of how the Old Testament points to the work of Christ.

All of our studies are designed with several things in mind:

1. **TO ADVANCE THE GOSPEL.**

    The Pew Research Center reports a rapidly changing religious landscape in the U.S., with the percentage of those identifying as atheist, agnostic, or "nothing in particular" up nine percent in just the last 10 years.[1] Almost 60 percent of our youth leave their churches as young adults, and this number is growing

    Despite this unsettling news, the core message of Christianity—the gospel—is still capable of renewing our lives and the church.

    Rather than worrying or acting out of fear and self-preservation, the best hope for Christians, the church, and people who feel pressure to abandon their faith is the historic Christian faith, the gospel announcement of what God has done through Jesus Christ for the world.

2. **TO SPEAK TO HONEST QUESTIONS.**

    Many in our evangelical, Baptist, Reformed, Lutheran, and Anglican churches have honest questions about faith and life that they may be afraid to ask. We shaped this study to address the concerns of long-time Christians, new Christians, Christians with wavering faith, and skeptics alike.

3. **TO ENGAGE THE DRAMA OF SCRIPTURE, TEACH THE DOCTRINE OF HISTORIC CHRISTIANITY, MOVE US TO DOXOLOGY (WORSHIP), AND ENABLE HEALTHY DISCIPLESHIP.**

    Our studies are written to show how doctrine naturally arises out of the Bible's narrative of Jesus Christ and his saving work. We designed the reflection and discussion questions with a practical emphasis to help you engage the material in a prayerful way that should inspire worship and lead to a fuller understanding of how to live as a disciple of Christ.

---

[1] Pew Research Center, "In U.S., Decline of Christianity Continues at Rapid Pace: An update on America's changing religious landscape," October 17, 2019, https://www.pewforum.org/2019/10/17/in-u-s-decline-of-christianity-continues-at-rapid-pace/.

4.   TO BE USEFUL IN A VARIETY OF SETTINGS.

We wrote this study thinking of Sunday school classes, Bible study groups, informal gatherings among friends, and individuals who want to learn more about the Christian faith. Each lesson includes a series of short sections containing a reading and a set of reflection questions. The leader's edition of this study has group discussion questions so that Christians can come together to share insights, ask questions, pray together, and be equipped to share what they're learning with friends and family.

We recommend you work through one lesson per week. If meeting with a group, we suggest reading the lesson and answering the questions on your own first.

"BUT JONAH ROSE TO FLEE TO TARSHISH

FROM THE PRESENCE OF THE LORD."

_____

Jonah 1:3

Fleeing *from* God

Read Jonah 1:1; Jeremiah 23:21–22; Hebrews 1:1–4

What's a Prophet?

Imagine you're in Israel in the eighth century BC. You're looking for work. You open the Jerusalem Daily News and an ad catches your eye: *Wanted—Prophet in Israel*. *Wow*, you think, *an opening for a prophet*. That's a big job. Everyone knows who the prophets are. You decide to check out the job requirements.

You see that, first, prophets need to be appointed by God. Lots of people pretend to be prophets (Jer. 23:21), but the Bible calls them false prophets. Authentic prophets are called by God himself. Next, the ad says a Hebrew prophet needs to have been in the divine council (Jer. 23:22; Isa. 6:1–4; Rev. 4:5–11). You imagine God enthroned in heaven, surrounded by angels—a heavenly courtroom. When God calls a prophet, the Holy Spirit brings him into God's presence to train him. The last requirement is anointing by God's Spirit (Num. 11:29). Prophets speak the word of God because the Holy Spirit fills them.

That's pretty daunting. It's probably not a great fit for you. But below the job qualifications you see the description of the job, so you keep reading, mainly out of curiosity. It says that a prophet is a preacher, lawyer, and fortune teller mixed together. That's an unpopular mix. Not only are you unqualified, but if you got the job, you'd probably lose all your friends.

Like preachers, prophets proclaim God's word. Throughout the Old Testament, God touches the mouths of the prophets when he calls them (Jer. 1:9; Isa. 6:6–7). Like lawyers, prophets prosecute people. They remind Israel of their covenant with God and how they've broken it. Like fortune tellers, prophets know the future. They tell God's people about coming blessings or curses.

In sum, prophets are messengers. They deliver messages from God.

A lot depends on messengers. When they don't do their job well, confusion and disaster can result. In modern times, we see it all the time. For example, in 2014, a flight vanished shortly after its take off in Jakarta, Indonesia. The families of the passengers waited weeks for news. When they finally heard something, it didn't come through a personal meeting or even a phone call. Instead, they got a text message saying, "Malaysia Airlines deeply regrets that we have to assume beyond any reasonable doubt that MH370 has been lost and that none of those aboard survived. As you will hear in the next hour from Malaysia's Prime Minister we must now accept that all evidence suggests the plane went down in the southern Indian Ocean."[1]

This struck many people as a cold and distant way to find out your relatives are dead. Even right information, if poorly delivered, can say something other than what you intend.

Imagine what it would be like to have to speak God's words on God's behalf. Imagine being given the job of communicating God's heart, will, and plan. No message could be more important. People's eternal souls are at stake. That's the prophet's task.

And that's Jonah's task. God calls him and anoints him with his Spirit. He's God's mouthpiece. God appoints him to the same role as any other prophet. Same requirements. Same job description.

---

[1] Steve Almasy, "Texts Fail When Delivering Tragic News, Experts Say," *CNN*, March 25, 2014, World, https://www.cnn.com/2014/03/25/world/asia/malaysia-airlines-text/index.html.

But Jonah, who hears from God and stands in his presence, wants a new job. As we'll see, he wants God to fire him.

The Ultimate Prophet

Do you know who else is a prophet? Jesus.

Jesus refers to himself as a prophet in Mark 6:4 and Luke 13:33. He's called by God (John 3:17; 17:18). As God the Son, he's always been in the divine council (John 1:1). The Holy Spirit anoints him (Luke 3:22). The book of Hebrews begins, "Long ago, at many times and in many ways, God spoke to our fathers by the prophets, but in these last days he has spoken to us by his Son" (Heb. 1:1–2). Jesus is the ultimate prophet.

And in Jesus, the messenger and the message become one: "the Word became flesh and dwelt among us" (John 1:14). Jesus is God's eternal Word (John 1:1).

Jonah, the rebel prophet, points to Jesus Christ. Jonah is a sinner like us, but his calling and message foreshadow what God would say through his Son hundreds of years later.

Questions for Reflection

1. What did you learn about the role of prophets in Israel that you didn't know before?

2. Prophets like Jonah don't exist today. But Christians look to the Bible the way Israel looked to the prophets. Why do you think that is?

Read Jonah 1:2; Ezekiel 33:8

What Message Did God Give to Jonah?

Jonah responds to God's call unlike any other prophet: he runs away, as we'll see in verse 3. But Jonah is also given a unique task. Rather than bearing a message for Israel, God's covenant people, God sends him to the pagan city Nineveh. This mission is something he probably never expected.

What does God want him to say to these gentiles?

Jonah 1:2 records no specific message. God says, "Arise, go to Nineveh, that great city, and call out against it, for their evil has come up before me." This command tells Jonah where to go, the kind of message to bring, and the reason for this mission.

Nineveh, which God calls "that great city" throughout Jonah (3:2; 4:11), was already ancient in Jonah's time. Genesis 10:11 mentions its founding. By the time of Jonah's calling, it was a major city in the Assyrian Empire. Not long after Jonah, Assyria conquered Israel and carried God's people into exile (2 Kings 17:5–6). The book of Jonah may have been written after the exile—no author or date is mentioned. But even in Jonah's lifetime, during the reign of Jeroboam in Israel (r. 786–746 BC), the Assyrian threat would've been clear.

God tells Jonah to "call out against" Nineveh. He tells Jonah to warn them of God's coming judgment. His message is bad news. But, as one commentator says, "The whole point of prophecy in Israel was to warn of impending judgment in order to encourage repentance and avert disaster."[2] A Hebrew prophet knows that God wants those who hear this kind of message to change course (Ezek. 33:8).

God tells Jonah to go because Nineveh's "evil has come up to me." God doesn't mention specifics, but Assyria was notoriously vicious. It provoked such terror that it often gained submission from other nations just by threatening them. One royal inscription says:

> By the command of Ashur (and) the goddess Ishtar, the great gods my lords, I moved out of the city Nineveh. . . . I approached the city Suru. . . . Awe of the radiance of Ashur my lord overwhelmed them. The nobles (and) elders of the city came out to me to save their lives. . . . I erected a pile in front of the gate; I flayed as many nobles as had rebelled against me (and) draped their skins over the pile. . . . I flayed many right through my land (and) draped their skins over the walls. . . . I brought Ahi-ababa [the ruler of Suru] to Nineveh, flayed him, (and) draped his skin over the wall of Nineveh."[3]

God doesn't tell Jonah why he's sending him to Nineveh at this specific time. But the sins of Assyria were obvious.

A Message of Judgment or Mercy?

Still, though, why would God send a Hebrew prophet? He'd never done that before. And according to the apostle Paul, all people already know that they're under God's judgment. After recording a long list of common human sins, Paul writes, "Though they know God's righteous decree that those who practice such things deserve to die, they not only do them but give approval to those who practice them" (Rom. 1:32). However foggy our understanding, we all know we've broken God's law. And we know we deserve to die.

God's purpose for Nineveh, then, must be something else. A message directly from God, in human words, is different. In fact, gentiles, though excluded from God's covenant with Israel, have an eternal stake in it.

---

[2] Kevin J. Youngblood, *Zondervan Exegetical Commentary on the Old Testament*, vol. 28, *Jonah*, ed. Daniel I. Block (Grand Rapids, MI: Zondervan, 2013), 54.

[3] Albert Kirk Grayson, *Assyrian Royal Inscriptions, vol. 2, From Tiglath-Pileser I to Ashur-nasir-apli II* (Wiesbaden, Germ.: Otto Harrassowitz, 1976), 123–124, quoted in Daniel C. Timmer, *A Gracious and Compassionate God: Mission, Salvation, and Spirituality in the Book of Jonah* (Downers Grove, IL: InterVarsity Press, 2011), 64.

A covenant, in a loose sense, is a legally established relationship. In the ancient world, strong kings made covenants with less powerful kings. The strong king promised to protect other kings in exchange for loyalty and service. The covenant included each party's duties and the penalties for not meeting those obligations. The parties bound themselves to these terms with an oath.

God's covenant with Israel, established on Mt. Sinai through Moses, defined his relationship with his people. God separated the Israelites from the rest of the nations as his own. He promised to bless them in extraordinary ways if they obeyed him. If they disobeyed, he'd punish them (Deut. 28). The prophets spoke to Israel in terms of this covenant, most often because of Israel's idolatry and other sins, warning them of God's coming wrath.

But the Mosaic covenant rested on a prior covenant that God made with Abraham. When God called Abraham, he said:

> Go from your country and your kindred and your father's house to the land that I will show you. And I will make you a great nation, and I will bless you and make your name great, so that you will be a blessing. I will bless those who bless you, and him who dishonors you I will curse, and in you all the families of the earth shall be blessed" (Gen. 12:2–3).

God fulfilled his promise to make Abraham "a great nation" when he formed Israel through the Mosaic covenant. But he also said that through Abraham "all the families of the earth shall be blessed." Through Israel, God planned to bless the whole world.

In this unprecedented call to Jonah, God seems to be doing something new. He's bringing his word to the gentiles, so that they might repent of their evil ways. The message of judgment may actually be a message of blessing. God remembers his promise to Abraham.

The Message of Freedom

When Jesus, Israel's Messiah, came, he called people to repent. But he did much more than that. On the cross, he submitted to all the curses of the Mosaic covenant to take away the sins of the world. Through Christ, God freed both Jews and gentiles from judgment forever.

In Christ, God fulfilled his promise to bless the nations and made a new covenant in his blood (Luke 22:20). After his resurrection, he sent messengers of this new covenant out into the world: "All authority in heaven and earth has been given to me. Go therefore and make disciples of all nations, baptizing them in the name of the Father and of the Son and of the Holy Spirit, teaching them to observe all that I have commanded you" (Matt. 28:28).

When God tells Jonah to go to Nineveh, he reminds Israel that he once told Abraham, centuries earlier, to "go" from his country and kinsmen. He gives a foretaste of the day when, centuries later, Jesus tells his disciples to "go" and bring good news to all the nations of the world.

Questions for Reflection

1. Why is Jonah's calling unique? Is the message God wants him to bring to Nineveh good news or bad news?

2. In some countries today, preaching the gospel is illegal and can even put your life in danger. In North America and Europe, this usually isn't the case, but we can still feel reluctant to share the message of Christ's death and resurrection. What do you find most difficult about sharing your faith with people?

Read Jonah 1:3; 2 Kings 14:25; Exodus 3:10

Why Does Jonah Run from God?

In Jonah, there's no story before God's call. No setting is described. The author mentions no year or season. He doesn't tell us who he is or why he's writing. He doesn't tell us anything about his main character, Jonah, except his name and his father's name. The word of God comes to Jonah, but we don't know where or how.

This differs from other prophets like Isaiah, Jeremiah, Ezekiel, and Daniel. Each of these books describe either a broad historical setting, the specific setting of God's call, or the prophet's life and background. It may be that the author of Jonah assumed that his audience would already be familiar with his protagonist.[4] Jonah is mentioned briefly in 2 Kings 14:25, where he spoke God's word to the evil king of Israel, Jeroboam. But since we don't know the author or when the book of Jonah was written, we also don't a have a clear sense of the book's original audience.

What matters is God's presence and call, not details about the prophet or setting. God is present, verses 1 and 2 show, through his word.

But geography appears in verse 3. Jonah doesn't say anything to God. Instead, he responds to his call by running away, with a particular geographical location in mind: "But Jonah rose to flee to Tarshish from the presence of the Lord" (Jon. 1:3). He's running away from God's calling, God's presence, and God's word.

---

[4] Bryan D. Estelle, *Salvation through Judgment and Mercy: The Gospel According to Jonah* (P&R Publishing: Phillipsburg, NJ, 2005), 12.

An Unprecedented Call

Jonah isn't the first reluctant prophet. Moses, Israel's first prophet, objected when God, speaking to him from a burning bush, called him to confront Pharaoh and lead God's people out of Egypt. He said, "Who am I that I should go to Pharaoh and bring the children of Israel out of Egypt?" (Exod. 3:10). Likewise, Jeremiah objected to his call, "Ah, Lord God! Behold, I do not know how to speak, for I am only a youth" (Jer. 1:6). Both question their own fitness for the task. In each case, God reassures them that he will be with them and give them the words to speak.

But Jonah doesn't say anything to God. Verse 3 doesn't offer any motive for Jonah's response. Nothing suggests he doubts his own abilities. No other prophet had ever run away from God's call, and the text doesn't say why he does this.

We know, though, where God has called him to go. Our geographical coordinates are Nineveh, northeast of Israel, and Tarshish, due west, across the Mediterranean Sea. God calls Jonah, like Moses, to speak to a great pagan empire. But Moses had grown up in Egypt, raised in Pharoah's family. And God called Moses to tell Pharaoh to let Israel go, so they could worship God in the land God had promised them through his covenant with Abraham (Gen. 15:18–21). It's a message of blessing and liberation for Moses' own people.

God calls Jonah, on the other hand, to leave the promised land and bring a message to a foreign empire. It's not a message of prosperity and freedom for Israel. In fact, Jonah likely knows it means the opposite. When idolatry and injustice characterized the monarchy in Israel, God brought acts of blessing to individual gentiles through his prophets, Elijah and Elisha (1 Kings 17:17–24; 2 Kings 5:1–14). According to Bryan D. Estelle, "There are, then, two sides to this coin. At the same time that blessings come to the gentiles, judgment comes upon Israel."[5] It's this unique calling that sends Jonah running.

The fact that we know little about Jonah also suggests that the problem is the task itself. No evidence indicates that Jonah had a prickly personality or a history of insubordination. It's not about Jonah—it's about the calling.

The Willing Prophet

It's likely, then, that Jonah points to something larger than himself. Though a historical figure, Jonah also represents the people of Israel. According to God's plan, all nations would know God through Israel's holy ways (1 Kings 8:59–6).[6] Jonah, fleeing from God's presence, is a picture of Israel. When God gives Jonah a message about the prosperity of his own people, Jonah listens and obeys (2 Kings 14:25). But he's utterly unwilling to bring the knowledge of God to a dangerous, pagan enemy.

Unlike Jonah, Jesus doesn't run from his call. He willingly comes to us. In fact, he becomes one of us. And he willingly goes to the cross, executed by a different pagan empire: "For this reason the Father loves me, because I lay down my life that I may take it up again. No one takes it from me, but I lay it down of my own accord. I have authority to lay it down, and I have authority to take it up again. This charge I received from my father" (John 10:17–18).

Jesus came willingly, so that we, through faith in him, could know God.

---

[5] Estelle, *Salvation through Judgment and Mercy*, 25.

[6] Estelle, *Salvation through Judgment and Mercy*, 23.

Questions for Reflection

1. Jonah likely represents the people of Israel. Why might this make sense? Are there ways in which he might represent God's people in all times and places?

2. When you think about Christ's willingness to serve you—to come into our world and our humanity and die for us—how does that affect you? What does it add to your grasp of the gospel?

"PERHAPS THE GOD WILL GIVE A THOUGHT

TO US, THAT WE MAY NOT PERISH."

Jonah 1:6

The *Sleeping* Prophet

Read Jonah 1:4; Psalm 107:23, 139:7

God Hunts Down Jonah

Jonah runs from the presence of God. Without a word, he flees in the opposite direction of Nineveh, where God commanded him to go. His motives aren't stated, but it's clear he finds his unique calling unacceptable. He's dead set against the will of God.

But how do you get away from God? He's present through his word. But God is also omnipresent—he's everywhere. He has no body, so no physical space confines him. When King Solomon dedicated the temple in Jerusalem, the building in which God would dwell among his people, he said, "But will God indeed dwell on the earth? Behold, heaven and the highest heaven cannot contain you; how much less this house that I have built!" (1 Kings 8:27). Jonah knew that God is everywhere, but now he faces it as a furious reality.

You've surely had bad days—days where it seems like everything goes wrong. As you try to fix one problem, you create another. You're backing out of the garage, late for a meeting, when you realize you forgot your wallet. Rushing into the house, you knock a mirror off the wall, which shatters when it hits the floor. Panicking, you impulsively grab a shard of glass and slice open the palm of your hand. Blood rains down on the carpet that was professionally cleaned the day before.

On bad days, we feel like there's a conspiracy against us. This much chaos must be organized. The world—or some invisible force—is actively, consciously against us.

For Jonah, starting in verse 4, this actually happens. The world is against him. All the elements oppose him. The conspiracy is real.

As the scene shifts from land to sea, God remains present. And God—not Jonah—controls the story: "But the Lord hurled a great wind upon the sea" (Jon. 1:4). Jonah doesn't run into some bad weather. God sends the wind and the storm. Commentators note that the unusual word order here in the Hebrew text, the subject coming before the verb, emphasizes God's orchestration of everything.[1] Even the ship "threatened to break up" (Jon. 1:4). The verb here personifies the ship.[2] It's like a conscious agent in the scene, threatening final disaster. The ship, like the weather, carries out God's will.

This helps us understand the scene, which lasts until the end of chapter 1: "Creation's conspiracy against Jonah fills this episode with irony . . . Thus creation serves as a messenger of divine wrath and a model of obedience to the divine call, both roles intended for Jonah."[3] When the prophet refuses God's call, God gives the prophet's task and message to nature. Jonah now receives the warning of coming judgment instead of bringing it.

No Escape From God's Call

Fleeing the call of God, you see, isn't possible. God didn't make Jonah a job offer. He didn't try to woo Jonah with paid sick days, a fitness center, and flexible work hours. Jonah has no choice. He's

---

[1] Timmer, *A Gracious and Compassionate God*, 68; Estelle, *Salvation through Judgment and Mercy*, 40.

[2] Estelle, *Salvation through Judgment and Mercy*, 41.

[3] Youngblood, *Jonah*, 73.

run away, but he's still called. As the apostle Paul says, "For the gifts and the calling of God are irrevocable" (Rom. 11:29). When God calls prophets—or anyone—he fulfills his plans for them.

Jonah's rebellion may feel familiar. We may defy God's will far more often than we dare admit. But in the face of this terrifying storm, there's hope for Jonah. And there's hope for us.

When the world seems to be against us and threatens the things we treasure, maybe even our lives, the knowledge that everything obeys God's will—that God's behind the conspiracy—can comfort us. Psalm 138:8 says, "The Lord will fulfill his purpose for me; your steadfast love, O Lord, endures forever." God, at times, sends what we most fear, so that we'll return to his presence in his word. There, we find his blessings and grace.

If he's called us, he won't let us get away.

Questions for Reflection

1. In what sense did Jonah flee God's presence? In what sense did he remain in God's presence?

2. Christians aren't Old Testament prophets, but if we've placed our trust in Christ and his death for our sins on the cross, we've been called by God. Whatever your theology, do you tend, in practice, to see your salvation as dependent on God's call or on your own efforts to be a good person?

Read Jonah 1:5; Romans 3:9–12

The Sleeper on the Pagan Ship

God's word came to Jonah, calling him to go to Nineveh (Jon. 1:1). Jonah responded by heading to Tarshish (Jon. 1:3). God then sent a storm to stop Jonah, showing his ultimate control of the story (1:4). Now, new characters respond to God. The storm terrifies the sailors, and fear pervades the rest of chapter 1. But during the panic on deck, Jonah the prophet—the object of God's wrath—remains below deck, asleep.

Jonah fled from God's presence. Yet God, who is everywhere, controls this new scene as much as he controlled the opening scene (Jon. 1:1–3). Through the mariners' response to the storm, we see the difference between God's presence throughout the world and his special presence through his word.

God doesn't speak to the sailors. They respond to the awesome effects of his presence, but they don't know what's going on. While they know the storm must have some source, they don't know what it is. So they call on their tribal deities: "Then the mariners were afraid, and each cried out to his own god" (Jon. 1:5).

But these sailors, who have a prophet aboard their ship, receive no answer to their cries for divine help.

The sailors, like Jonah, deserve God's wrath. They're idolators, seeking salvation through false gods (Rom. 3:9–12).[4] But the author, by contrasting the sailors with Jonah, makes them sympathetic. They've done nothing to cause this particular storm. Their lives are endangered because of Jonah. They're helpless, ignorant, and terrified. We feel their desperation and pity them. The author contrasts the sailors and Jonah throughout the chapter, using irony to deepen our sense of Jonah's folly.

Hearing no answer to their prayers, the sailors "hurled the cargo that was in the ship into the sea to lighten it for them" (Jon. 1:5). They do what they can to save themselves. The author uses the same verb here, "hurled," that he used in verse 4 to describe God sending the wind. While God can do whatever he wills, though, the sailors' tossing of cargo overboard is futile. If God wants to sink the ship, no efforts to make it more buoyant will matter.

The Sleeping Prophet

Jonah, meanwhile, sleeps inside the ship. The pandemonium doesn't disturb him. Why? The author refers to the sailors' fear throughout the chapter. But he never says Jonah is afraid. If God's wrath is against him, why isn't he afraid? Is his sleep a kind of defiance?

We're not told directly, but commentators note that Jonah moves "down" throughout chapter 1. He "went down to Joppa," "down into" the ship (1:3), and then "down into the inner part of the ship" (1:5). And if the ship comes apart, his downward journey will continue. Jonah wanted to go west to Tarshish, but instead he's heading in a different direction.

He may be well aware of this. The contrast between the sailors' struggle to survive and the prophet's hibernation may show that Jonah "resigns himself to death."[5] Other evidence seems to support this idea. First, Scripture at times refers to death as "sleep." For example, Psalm 13:3 says, "Consider and answer me, O Lord my God; light up my eyes, lest I sleep the sleep of death." The author of Jonah may also want us to make this association.

More importantly, though, Jonah knows God. He's a prophet called to bring a message of judgment to an evil nation. He knows that defiance of God results in death. There's good reason, then, to think Jonah expects to die. He's run from an intolerable call, but he knows he's a dead man walking.

Jonah's sleep also emphasizes his dereliction of duty. He's on a ship full of pagan idolators, the kind of people God told him to warn. They're desperate for revelation—a divine response to their cries. Yet the prophet on board is snoozing.

---

[4] Estelle, *Salvation through Judgment and Mercy*, 42.

[5] Youngblood, *Jonah*, 70.

The Sleeping Savior

In some of its main features, this scene resembles the story of Jesus sleeping during the storm on the sea of Galilee, recorded in Matthew 8:23–27, Mark 4:35–41, and Luke 8:22–25:

> On that day, when evening had come, he said to them, "Let us go across to the other side." And leaving the crowd, they took him with them in the boat, just as he was. And other boats were with him. And a great windstorm arose, and the waves were breaking into the boat, so that the boat was already filling. But he was in the stern, asleep on the cushion. And they woke him and said to him, "Teacher, do you not care that we are perishing?" And he awoke and rebuked the wind and said to the sea, "Peace! Be still!" And the wind ceased, and there was a great calm. He said to them, "Why are you so afraid? Have you still no faith?" And they were filled with great fear and said to one another, "Who then is this, that even the wind and the sea obey him?" (Mark 4:35–41)

In both stories, a prophet on a ship sleeps during a storm. In both, fear overwhelms the other sailors. In neither story do the sailors know who controls the storm. They don't know who has the power to save them.

But while Jonah's sleep defies the will of God, Jesus's sleep results from peace with it.[6] And while Jonah knew God and could have called out to him to calm the storm, Jesus, the Son of God, controls the wind and the waves. The prophet in the boat on the sea of Galilee could end the storm with his words.

Questions for Reflection

1. Those who don't know Christ can provoke both our righteous anger and our deep compassion. For example, in the story of Jonah, we might feel like the violence of the Assyrians is intolerable but feel sympathy for the sailors in the storm. Do you find it hard to hate sin while at the same time feeling compassion for sinners? If so, why do you think that is?

2. In the passage from the Gospel of Mark quoted above, Jesus seems to contrast fear with faith. How do you think fear and faith relate to each other? What do you think explains Jonah's sleeping during the storm?

---

[6] Estelle, *Salvation through Judgment and Mercy*, 45–46.

Read Jonah 1:6

The Silent Prophet

Although the storm doesn't wake Jonah up, the captain of the ship does when he finds him below deck. In words that unwittingly echo God's call, the captain confronts Jonah with an urgent concern for salvation.

When the captain finds Jonah, he says, "What do you mean, you sleeper?" (Jon. 1:6). In other words, he's saying, *What's your problem, slacker?* The lives of everyone on board are at risk, but Jonah is doing nothing. He's supposed to bring a rebuke to the pagans, but this pagan rebukes him. We, of course, know it's even worse than the captain realizes. This "sleeper" has caused the storm that threatens their lives.

These are the first words spoken by a human in the book of Jonah. The prophet called by God to speak hasn't said anything yet. The captain's words are the first words since God spoke to Jonah in 1:2. And he calls Jonah to action, just as God did: "Arise, call out to your god!" (Jon. 1:6) As one commentator points out, the captain's commands, "Arise" and "call out," echo God's commands to Jonah: "Arise, go to Nineveh, that great city, and call out against it" (Jon. 1:2).[7] Jonah hears God's call again, in the bowels of the ship.[8]

The captain commands him to call out to his god. Jonah, like everyone else, should do his part by calling out to whatever local deity he worships. If you call out to enough gods, you might find one with jurisdiction over the storm. "Perhaps," he says, "the god will give a thought to us, that we may not perish" (Jon. 1:6). He assumes Jonah is a pagan like the rest of the crew.

Yet again, though, readers of the story understand something the captain doesn't. We know that the captain has found the right man. Jonah's God isn't just another god in the Rolodex. He's the God who hurled down the wind that threatens their lives. He's the only true and living God, the only one who can save them.

We also know that Jonah *ought* to be calling out to his God instead of sleeping. The sailors cry out in their ignorance. They don't know which god is willing and able to save them. They don't know the source of their trouble or the solution to it.[9] But Jonah knows God. He can cry out with confidence, because he knows what God is like. He could reveal all this to the captain. But instead of identifying himself as a prophet of God, his only identity is "sleeper."

Rebuking God's Prophets

This verse suggests another similarity to the story of Jesus in the storm. Their fellow sailors, not the storm, wake up both Jesus and Jonah. And the sailors rebuke both prophets. The disciples say to Jesus, "Teacher, do you not care that we are perishing?" (Mark 4:38). They thought they knew him, but his slumber seemed like a lack of concern for their lives. Both Jesus and Jonah hear, upon waking, *What's your problem? Why don't you care about what's happening?*

---

[7] Youngblood, *Jonah*, 76.

[8] Youngblood, *Jonah*, 76.

[9] Youngblood, *Jonah*, 67.

But while Jonah stays silent, Jesus speaks. He tells the storm, "Peace! Be Still!" (Mark 4:39) And having brought calm, he responds with a rebuke of his own: "Why are you so afraid? Have you still no faith?" (Mark 4:40). The disciples' accusatory tone reflects their lack of faith. The captain, too, lacks faith in the true God, but he justly accuses Jonah of sleeping on the job.

Later, Jonah also calms the sea, but in a different way. And this will remind us of another moment in the ministry of Jesus. When Jonah is hurled into the ocean, his descent points to the deeper descent of Jesus—into the tomb. Through his death, Jesus stills the storm of God's wrath forever.

Questions for Reflection

1. Has someone who wasn't a Christian ever justly accused you of not living in a way that fits with the gospel? What, in particular, do you think God may want to teach us in those kinds of situations?

2. Can you think of times when identifying yourself as a Christian would have benefitted people, but you stayed silent about your faith? If so, what did you feel it would have cost you to speak?

"FOR THE MEN KNEW THAT HE WAS FLEEING

FROM THE PRESENCE OF THE LORD."

Jonah 1:10

"What *Is* This You Have Done!"

Read Jonah 1:7; 2 Corinthians 5:21

Who's to Blame?

Have you ever been in a situation where someone else's actions could have gotten you in trouble?

When I was in college, I lived in a rough neighborhood with a group of Christian friends. The rent was extremely cheap and the neighborhood offered a lot of opportunities for ministry. We got to know the kids on our street really well. A lot of them came from troubled homes and had dropped out of high school. We'd often hang out with them on our front stairs.

One night, we sat out front with about five of these kids, talking about the gospel. They drank and smoked while we talked, but they were willing to listen to us. They were somber, because we were talking about God's judgment.

Then a guy rushed up, pushing a shopping cart full of stuff. I couldn't tell what was in the cart, but he had a big smile on his face. He said, "I just broke into Chase Elementary School and stole all of these overhead projectors!" He went on and on about how much money they were worth and how easy they were to steal. He just needed a place to store them.

Then he looked at me and my roommates and said, "Can I store them here?"

He had no idea what we'd just been talking about, and he looked baffled when everyone stayed quiet. No one seemed to share his excitement. As someone training for the ministry, my first thought was, *It sure would be nice to have a projector or two.* But my second thought was, *There's no way I'm going to let this guy in my house with these stolen goods.* I didn't want to get in trouble for this kid's crime.

If he'd been as clever as Jonah, he might have concealed the fact that he'd stolen the projectors. Then, we might have let him in. And the police, who found him about an hour later, might also have arrested my roommates and me.

The sailors on the boat with Jonah the prophet don't know it, but they're accomplices to a crime. Jonah has broken God's law. God commands people to serve him alone, but Jonah has chosen to serve himself. God is hunting down his renegade prophet, and these sailors have been helping Jonah flee.

At this point, the sailors know someone's guilty of something. They've cried out to their gods and received no answer. They've thrown their cargo into the ocean to lighten the ship. But they're still fighting for their lives in the furious storm. Someone, they know, has done something to make some god mad. But that's all they know. They don't know who to blame.

What Will Reveal the Truth?

They're desperate for information. They want to know how to save their ship. So, they decide to cast lots: "And they said to one another, 'Come, let us cast lots, that we may know on whose account this evil has come upon us'" (Jon. 1:7). Casting lots is like drawing straws or consulting the magic 8-ball. Do you remember the magic 8-balls that you could shake to find out your future? They would tell you, *outlook good* or *seems doubtful.* That's basically what the sailors do.

Deuteronomy 18:9–14 calls divinization—occult techniques for seeking divine revelation—"abominable practices." It was associated with idolatry and witchcraft. But casting lots was acceptable. In fact, in the New Testament, the apostles cast lots to choose Judas' replacement, Matthias (Acts 1:26). God was willing at that time to use lots in order to guide his people. Here, he uses them to make known the truth to the sailors.

"So they cast the lots, and the lot fell on Jonah" (Jon. 1:7). Jonah, against his will, has been revealed. We can imagine the eyes of everyone going to the silent man who entered the ship at Joppa. The sleeper.

This man is a prophet who knows God's will. All along he's known the cause of the storm. He's known how the storm could be brought to an end. But he's been silent. He hasn't given the sailors the revelation they desperately need. He hasn't called out to his God. And in this way, he's brought these sailors to the brink of death. He's drawn them into his crime and the judgment it deserves.

Entangled in Sin

Now, God—through the lots—has revealed Jonah as the cause of this disaster. He's giving these men the chance to walk away from what they're entangled in.

In the big picture, though, we're all entangled in the sin of Adam, both Jew and gentile alike (Rom. 3:9–11). The sailors didn't cause the storm, but they're as guilty before God as Jonah. This storm, in fact, is a picture that points us to the final judgment. At the end of time, God will judge every crime and execute perfect justice.

But God has provided us with a way of escape. Jesus, the second Adam, chose to take the blame for our crimes: "For our sake he made him to be sin who knew no sin, so that in him we might become the righteousness of God" (2 Cor. 5:21). Jesus never sinned, nor was he an accomplice to sin. But he associated himself with our crimes. He came, in fact, to take the blame.

Questions for Reflection

1. Why do you think the sailors conclude that someone must have done something to cause the storm? Why would they think it has something to do with human guilt?

2. What are some ways that non-Christians you know seek revelation? What do they trust to reveal the source of their troubles or their future outlook?

Read Jonah 1:8–9; Romans 8:5–10

Who Is Jonah?

Imagine the sailors on the deck in a big circle, sheets of water coming over the ship's sides. These men have been fighting for their lives, and they're desperate to discover the source of the calamity that's come upon them. So they cast lots, and the lots point towards Jonah.

After this, it's one irony after another until the end of the chapter.

An irony is a situation that's strange, funny, or even tragic because things play out contrary to your expectations. It's ironic to see a student instructing a professor. It's ironic to see a firetruck on fire or a mouse chasing a cat.

Irony #1: What Is Your Occupation?

We see the first irony in verse 8, when the sailors ask, "What is your occupation?" Of course, we—the readers—already know the answer. He's a prophet. He's supposed to bring a message from God. But he's not doing his job very well. Imagine a pastor in a place he shouldn't be—in the middle of a fist fight or a drug deal. Someone asks him, "Hey, what do you do for work?" If he says, "I'm a pastor," he's going to confuse people. That's not where he's supposed to be.

These sailors probably think that whatever Jonah does for work must be pretty bad. Maybe he's a professional thief or an assassin. He's obviously made some god very, very upset. But Jonah doesn't answer this first question. Maybe he's embarrassed.

Irony #2: "I Fear the Lord"

We see the next irony in Jonah's response. The prophet, here in verse 9, speaks for the first time in the book named after him. He says, "I am a Hebrew, and I fear the Lord" (Jon. 1:9). This sounds like an orthodox confession of faith. It may confirm the idea that Jonah represents Israel.[1] But Jonah is fleeing from God and hiding the truth about who he is and what he's done. While the terrified sailors have rushed around trying to survive, Jonah hasn't shown any sign of fear. But he says, "I fear the Lord, the God of heaven" (Jon. 1:9). His words and actions don't line up.

This irony tells us something vital about Jonah. However rebellious his actions may be, he sees himself as one who fears God. He's probably not lying to them. He won't admit that he's a prophet, but he doesn't hide his ethnic identity. He's one of God's chosen people. To be a Hebrew is to be one who fears the Lord. This is the source of his pride, his self-worth.

People often say, "Those Christians are hypocrites. They say one thing and do something else." Sometimes, people just want a reason to reject God. But here, Jonah is saying he fears God only shows us that he doesn't fear God, because his actions say something else.

We've all talked to people who say, "I love God," but their lives tell a different story. In Titus 1:16, the apostle Paul says of certain people, "They profess to know God, but they deny him by their works."

---

[1] Estelle, *Salvation through Judgment and Mercy*, 50.

He calls them "empty talkers" (Tit. 1:10). That's Jonah in this scene. His speech is hollow.

Irony #3: Fleeing by Sea

Jonah's response also reveals a third irony. He says, "I fear the Lord, the God of heaven, who made the sea and the dry land" (Jon. 1:9). Jonah is on the run. He's fleeing from God's presence. Yet, he's fleeing by sea from the God who made the sea. He's fleeing the God who's everywhere. The gentile sailors have been frantically calling out to their local gods for deliverance, but Jonah, the Hebrew, knows the one God, the creator of the world. With the God of Israel, there's nowhere to run and nowhere to hide.

Irony #4: The Silent Prophet Prophesies

A fourth irony is that God has forced Jonah to prophesy.[2] It's not, at this point, his original calling to Nineveh. But here on the ship with these gentiles, God has left Jonah no way out. When the lots reveal him as the one to blame, he has to say something about himself. He's telling gentiles the message God wants them to hear about how they can save their lives. Despite making every effort to escape his calling, Jonah fulfills it, and his own identity is what's revealed.

What About You?

Does the world need to ask you your occupation? Is it a secret that you follow the true God? When you say, "I fear the Lord," do you say it like Jonah did? Are those hollow words? Is the reality that you live for yourself and fear people? Do you say you fear God while you're actually disobeying him? Do you act as though you can flee from his presence, even though he made the sea and the dry land? Are you unwilling to let go of certain sins in your life?

If so, then, like Jonah, you're on an impossible path. It's a path that can only lead to death.

But if we're Christians, then Christ—God's eternal Word—lives inside us through his Holy Spirit. We can never be away from his presence, no matter how we feel. We belong to him and find our identity in him. And through his Spirit, he grants us repentance, so we can turn from our sins and live.

There's an irony in the sinless Son of God dying like a criminal. It's not what anyone would ever expect. It's the irony God uses to confound—and save—the world.

---

[2] Youngblood, *Jonah*, 77.

Questions for Reflection

1 . What does Jonah seem to see as his main identity? Are there ways we can misunderstand what it means to be a Christian? If so, how?

2 . We often associate irony with humor. Things are often funny because they go against what we expect. Is there anything funny about this scene? Would humor be out of place in a story about such dire circumstances? Can humorous irony ever help us see a serious point more clearly?

Read Jonah 1:10; Genesis 20:1–11

What the Pagans Know

When Jonah reveals his identity, the fear that's driven the sailors only ramps up. Jonah knows "the God of heaven, who made the sea and the dry land" (Jon. 1:9). This is no tribal deity. They're dealing with a whole other level of divine power.

This tragic irony is too much for the sailors to bear: "Then the men were exceedingly afraid and said to him, 'What is this that you have done!'" (Jon. 1:10) In other words, they say, *You're fleeing by sea from the God who controls the sea? You, Hebrew, who say you fear God, can you outrun the wind and the waves? Are you going to evade God in his own domain?* The sailors are astounded. This isn't one of the gods they'd been calling out to for salvation. This isn't the wind god or the rain god. This is the God of gods. That's who Jonah, the Hebrew, has offended.

This is the second accusation against Jonah from the pagans. In verse 6, the captain found Jonah sleeping inside the ship and said, "What do you mean, you sleeper?" Now they know Jonah's identity and the cause of the storm. They're getting closer to the truth, and the accusation gets closer to the heart of the matter.

A Familiar Accusation

An accusation like this appears several other times in the Old Testament.[3] God asks Eve, "What is this that you have done?" (Gen. 3:13) after she eats the forbidden fruit. He asks Cain the same

---

[3] Youngblood, *Jonah*, 79

question after he kills his brother, Abel (Gen. 4:10). The sailors' expression of shock echoes the response of God to these archetypal human sins. It may be, then, that we should see Jonah's sin as being just as grievous as Eve's or Cain's—or the Assyrians'.

This accusation also appears in three scenes in which, like this one, pagans uncover the sin of God's people (Gen. 12:18; 20:9; 26:10). In each case, Abraham or Isaac fears a pagan ruler and lies to save his life. By doing so, they put the pagans at risk of guilt and judgment. In fact, God sends plagues upon the Egyptians Abraham has deceived, a foreshadowing of the Exodus (Gen. 12:17). When the rulers discover the truth, in each case they say, "What is this you have done to us?"

The Humiliated Prophet

If nothing else, these verses all show that God's people have no natural moral superiority. Apart from the grace of God, they're no better than pagans. Here, in the case of Jonah, we're reminded that this can be true even in terms of religious faith.

Solomon, who built God's temple, introduced idol worship into Israel (1 Kings 11:6–8). Through Solomon, then, Israel broke the Mosaic covenant. As a consequence, God divided Israel into separate northern and southern kingdoms (1 Kings 11:9–13). Idolatry continued under many subsequent kings and at times even included human sacrifice (2 Kings 16:3; 17:17–18). These practices, in fact, caused God to send the Assyrians to overthrow the northern kingdom of Israel and bring God's people into exile (2 Kings 17:6). They end up living under the rule of the very people Jonah refuses to warn.

In Jonah's time, King Jeroboam II was "evil" and "did not depart from all the sins of Jeroboam the son of Nebat, which he made Israel to sin" (2 Kings 14:24). This earlier Jeroboam, the first ruler of the northern kingdom, instituted idol worship in order to establish his power (1 Kings 12:27–29). He erected numerous religious sites as alternatives to the temple in Jerusalem (1 Kings 12:31). Jeroboam II, Jonah's king, is like him. This likely means that idolatry was flourishing in Israel in Jonah's time.

The sailors may not know all the details of Jonah's story. It's not clear what exactly he reveals. But they know, at least, that running from the presence of this great God is an egregious evil: "For the men knew that he was fleeing from the presence of the Lord, because he had told them" (Jon. 1:10). This rebuke from the pagans *should* be an astounding humiliation for Jonah. Most likely, that's God's intention.

Even the pagans can see that Jonah has done something stunningly wicked. And, in fact, things back home in idolatrous Israel aren't much better. Jonah, as we've said, most likely represents Israel. The author of Jonah probably wants to remind God's people of their sin. He wants them to remember that they have more in common with the pagans than they'll admit. And that God established his covenant with them by grace alone.

To our shame, the world often uncovers the sins of the church. At times, unbelievers have a moral clarity God's people lack. Rather than digging in our heels and defending ourselves, we're called at these times to repent. As we honestly confess our sin and entrust ourselves to God's grace, we reveal our true identity to the watching world.

Questions for Reflection

1. Is Jonah's sin as bad as the Assyrians'? Why or why not? What do you think the author wants us to believe?

2. What is repentance? What role does it play in the Christian life?

Notes

"THEN THE MEN FEARED THE LORD

EXCEEDINGLY, AND THEY OFFERED A

SACRIFICE TO THE LORD AND MADE VOWS."

Jonah 1:16

The Sailors vs. *The* Sea

Read Jonah 1:11–12; Leviticus 7:1–6; Hebrews 9:11–15

Jonah Offers His Life

Through the unwilling revelation of his prophet, God has revealed to the sailors the source of their trouble. But they're not out of danger. Instead, their fear only grows as they learn that Jonah has offended a God of more extraordinary power than they'd imagined.

Now, they need to know what they're supposed to do.

Only Jonah, who has brought disaster on the ship, knows the God they're dealing with. So, the sailors ask him, "What shall we do to you, that the sea may quiet down for us?" (Jon. 1:11). *How do we appease this God? How do we satisfy his anger? What payment does he require?* Jonah is the cause of their problems. He's also the solution to their problems. It's Jonah's God who's about to destroy them.

At the same time, the storm's threat only grows: "For the sea grew more and more tempestuous" (Jon. 1:11). As the sailors get closer to the truth, the world around them only gets more dangerous.

Jonah says to them, "Pick me up and hurl me into the sea" (Jon. 1:12). Commentators disagree about Jonah's motives here. Has he had a change of heart? Does he feel compassion for the sailors? Or does he just want to die?[1]

As we've seen, there are good reasons to think Jonah has resigned himself to death. His physical movement down throughout chapter 1 seems to be leading to an eventual descent into the sea. He knows the consequences of defying God. He knows he deserves to die.

What Jonah doesn't say here may also help. It gives us a glimpse into his heart. He doesn't say, "Let's turn around and go back to Joppa." He doesn't say, "Let me pray and ask God to forgive me for what I've done." The other sailors ran around in a frenzy calling out to their gods (Jon. 1:5). The captain woke up Jonah and ordered him to call out to his god (Jon. 1:6). But Jonah has refused to call out.

And Jonah still refuses to call out to his God. He'd rather be thrown into the sea. He'd rather die than talk to God.

Jonah offers his life to save the ship, but it's a pseudo-sacrifice. If he'd rather die than bring God's word to the gentile Ninevites, should we think he wants to give his life for pagan sailors? He hasn't cared about them until now, and nothing suggests he would ever have said anything if the lots—by God's hand—hadn't revealed Jonah as the cause of the storm (Jon. 1:7).

So, if Jonah suddenly has compassion on the sailors, what evidence supports this?

It's more likely that Jonah sees there's no way out. He's been revealed. The sailors demand an answer. And there's no escape from Yahweh. It may look like a sacrifice, but it isn't. In fact, rather than an

---

[1] Estelle, *Salvation through Judgment and Mercy*, 56.

act of love, it's an act of hatred. He could repent and return to land, but he refuses. It's a completely unnecessary "sacrifice." It's part of his unwillingness to bring God's word to gentiles.

Unwillingness to repent always ends with death. Jonah won't let go of his sin, so he must die.

The True Sacrifice

When the sailors ask, "What shall we do to you, so that the sea may quiet down for us?" (Jon. 1:11), they seem to know some kind of propitiation is necessary in this situation. Something needs to be done to appease Jonah's God. They assume something needs to be done to the culprit, but they don't know what.

Both Jews and gentiles offered sacrifices. The sacrifices offered by Israel were those God had commanded in the Mosaic covenant. Through these sacrifices, Israel made peace with God. But the blood of animals couldn't make a lasting atonement with God. Instead, these offerings pointed to a future sacrifice. When Jesus came, he "entered once for all into the holy places, not by means of the blood of goats and calves but by means of his own blood, thus securing an eternal redemption" (Heb. 9:12). Jesus came to offer his life. This was the only sacrifice that could truly appease God.

Even if Jonah had wanted to give his life to save the sailors, all he could do was save them from a storm. As a sinner himself, he couldn't take away their sin. Even if his motives were righteous and pure, if this was a noble self-sacrifice, it could only point to another.

Jonah deserves the death he expects here. But centuries after Jonah, the God of heaven, who made the sea and the dry land, sent his Son. He went down to a death he didn't deserve; when he offered himself, it was a true sacrifice. He died for the sins of people like you and me—Jews and gentiles, Jonah and the sailors.

Questions for Reflection

1. As you study these verses in the context of the first chapter as a whole, what do you think leads Jonah to tell the sailors to throw him overboard? Do you think there are reasons to see it as an act of love?

2. Are there certain sins in your life that you've found difficult to repent of? If so, why do you think it's so hard for you to let them go?

Read Jonah 1:13; Romans 8:31–39

The Pagans Try to Save Jonah

Jonah's reasons for offering up his life aren't immediately clear. And the sailors' response to his suggestion isn't easy to explain either: "Nevertheless, the men rowed hard to get back to dry land" (Jon. 1:13). They know Jonah has caused the danger they're in. They believe he knows the God who brought the storm. They've been seeking a revelation—the knowledge of how they can placate the divine wrath and survive. They asked Jonah what to do and, his hand being forced, he told them.

So, why don't they just throw him in? Is it sympathy for Jonah? Do they row toward land out of kindness? Are they more merciful than Jonah, the prophet of God, who until now would have been happy for them all to drown?

Or are they worried they'd get in trouble with the law? But couldn't they easily say he fell overboard in the terrible storm?

Their main motive seems to be revealed when they cry out to God in verse 14, saying, "Let us not perish for this man's life." They know they're being watched by an extraordinarily powerful God. Throwing Jonah into the sea is an extreme solution. It might be murder, and this God will see it. So, they won't do it because they know the consequences may be exactly what they want to avoid—their own deaths.

So, the suspense of the sailors—and us, if our sympathy is with them—only grows as they set themselves against the storm. They're going to try to find another way, through their own efforts.

The Sea against the Sailors

Yet the men have received a revelation from God. And they, like Jonah, find nature conspiring against them when they begin rowing for land: "Nevertheless, the men rowed hard to get back to dry land, but they could not, for the sea grew more and more tempestuous against them" (Jon. 1:13). The last phrase mimics verse 11: "For the sea grew more and more tempestuous." But now the author adds, "against them." As he did in verse 4, the author personifies the inanimate elements. The sea grows stormier *against* the sailors. God's conspiracy continues: "YHWH's creational conspiracy permits no human solutions. The elements oppose the mariners until they to join YHWH's conspiracy."[2] God will cause the sailors, also, to submit to his will.

God will fulfill his purposes. No human scheme or effort can stop him.

But for God's people, this is our great comfort. The apostle Paul writes, "For I am sure that neither death nor life, nor angels nor rulers, nor things present nor things to come, nor powers, nor height nor depth, nor anything else in all creation, will be able to separate us from the love of God in Christ Jesus our Lord" (Rom. 8:38–39).

All creation has been against Jonah. In this verse, creation is against the sailors. But why? What is God's plan for them? Could these forces of nature that seem ready to separate them from God forever actually be God's way of preserving them?

---

[2] Youngblood, *Jonah*, 83.

Questions for Reflection

1. What do you think best explains the sailors' actions in this verse? What does the evidence in the text seem to suggest?

2. At this point in the story, is God's plan becoming clear? Are there clues that tell us what God wants to happen to Jonah and the sailors?

Read Jonah 1:14–16; Romans 3:21–26

Missionary Success?

The sailors' efforts to get to land are futile. They've now tried everything. Clearly, this God who rules the sea has left them no other options. For the first time, they cry out to the God of Jonah: "Therefore, they called out to the Lord" (Jon. 1:14). God's conspiracy has led them to put their trust in him.

This scene ends, then, with a final irony. Jonah, the prophet of Yahweh, won't call out to his God. But the sailors, who had earlier been calling out to their pagan gods, now cry out to the God of Jonah: "O Lord, let us not perish for this man's life, and lay not on us innocent blood, for you, O Lord, have done as it pleased you" (Jon. 1:14). Jonah had told them, "I am a Hebrew, and I fear the Lord" (Jon. 1:9). But it's these gentiles now who actually fear the Lord.

You can hear the fear in their voices as they cry out to the Lord for the first time. Jonah the prophet hasn't spoken to God once yet in this story. When Jonah spoke, because he had no choice, he spoke only to the sailors. And he said, essentially, *Let me die.* The sailors' prayer is the opposite of Jonah's wish. They say, *O God, please don't let us die.* God doesn't shut his ears to any human being, Jew or gentile, who calls upon him in truth.

A New Kind of Fear

The sailors do what Jonah asks: "So they picked up Jonah and hurled him into the sea" (Jon. 1:15). Their actions, now that they've submitted to God's will, are effective: "and the sea ceased from its raging" (Jon. 1:15).

This means that the words of Jonah prove true. He's a rebel prophet, but he's still a real prophet. In spite of every effort to escape his calling, he reveals what God wants him to reveal in this scene. God causes everything to work against Jonah, pinning him to the mat. Now, the sea ceases to express God's wrath. The conspiracy succeeds.

The end of the storm creates a new kind of fear in the sailors: "Then the men feared the Lord exceedingly" (Jon. 1:16). It's not the fear of the wind or drowning, not the fear of death, but the fear of the Lord. It's similar to what the disciples felt when Jesus ended the storm on the Sea of Galilee: "And they were filled with great fear and said to one another, 'Who then is this, that even the wind and the sea obey him?'" (Mark 4:41). The terror caused by the storm gives way to a greater fear. They're in the presence of someone whose power exceeds anything in nature.

The men now make a sacrifice, but it's not Jonah: "and they offered a sacrifice to the Lord and made vows" (Jon. 1:16). Throughout Scripture, God's people make sacrifices to show their devotion to him, even before the covenant with Moses (Gen. 4:2–4; 8:20). By believing God's revelation, fearing him, calling on his name, and offering sacrifices, they act like those who belong to the true God—those who have come into his presence.

Has Jonah, even as he sinks into the sea, achieved missionary success? Has God used him against his will to bring salvation to these gentiles? That seems to be the case. By offering up himself, he saved them, regardless of his motives. He told them who the true God is. Now, the sailors are safe and worshiping the God of Israel. But is Jonah lost?

Questions for Reflection

1.   Can you think of a time when God has brought good into your life, despite every effort to achieve the opposite? If you remember your conversion, would you describe it as a result of your search for God—or did God seem to draw you to himself in spite of all your efforts to avoid him?

2.   When you read about God working through sinners, how does this affect your view of his character? Would he seem holier and more glorious if he worked through virtuous heroes?

"OUT OF THE BELLY OF SHEOL I CRIED,

AND YOU HEARD MY VOICE."

Jonah 2:2

Jonah *in the* Fish

Read Jonah 1:17; 1 Corinthians 15:12–19

God Calls a Fish

Jonah has been heading down since this story began. Now, beneath the peaceful surface of the sea, he's sinking. While the gentile sailors worship the one true God, the prophet goes down, it seems, to the death he deserves.

Yet God calls another creature into his service. When Jonah fled his calling, God appointed the wind and the sea as his servants. Now, he calls a fish. "And the Lord appointed a great fish to swallow up Jonah. And Jonah was in the belly of the fish three days and three nights" (Jon. 1:17). Although Jonah deserves to die, God sends a fish to save him by consuming him.

History or Fiction?

At this point, a question may come to your mind. Is this historical? Did this actually happen? Did some guy really live in a fish for three days?

In our time, we often separate history and literature. We see that the book of Jonah is story. We see that dramatic, unusual things happen and that it's carefully structured to make moral and theological points. Clearly, we may think, this is fiction. It's like one of Aesop's fables. It uses an engaging narrative to teach moral and "spiritual" truths. Of course, we're not supposed to take it literally, right?

But ancient writers didn't separate history and literature as neatly as we do. Stories about real events could be crafted in ways that draw attention to theology or whatever the writer believes is important. Stories could be highly stylized, and also true. The literary qualities in Jonah—its narrative structure, use of irony, fabulous occurrences, and, as we'll see, poetry—shouldn't lead us to conclude that the story is made up.

We also shouldn't conclude it's fiction because, we may think, *this could never happen. Obviously a guy can't survive in a fish for three days. They probably believed stuff like that back then, but now we know how the world really works.* The philosopher Alvin Plantinga calls this general attitude "as-we-now-knowism."[1]

But if you believe in a God who created all things and the natural laws that govern them, why couldn't that same God disrupt the laws of nature when he wants to? When we're wondering if miracles are possible, we're asking about the nature of God. Is God omnipotent or not? Christians, Jews, and Muslims have always believed he is. The Bible claims that God is almighty (Gen.1:17; Rev. 4:8). If he is, then he can perform miracles.

As Christians, our faith rests on the reality of miracles. Jesus performed miracles during his ministry as signs that proved he was God in the flesh. Christian faith, according to the apostle Paul, depends on a miracle. Jesus Christ lay dead in the ground for three days. Then he returned to life. If this didn't happen, Paul says, "Your faith is futile and you are still in your sins" (1 Cor. 15:17).

If God is all-powerful, he can do the miraculous. If we believe in the biblical God, we can believe a

---

[1] Alvin Plantinga, "Christian Philosophy at the End of the Twentieth Century," in *The Analytic Theist: an Alvin Plantinga Reader*, ed. James F. Sennett (Grand Rapids: Eerdmans, 1998), 328.

man can live in a fish for three days. And if we're Christians, we must believe in miracles. Our faith and our salvation depend on it.

But we still might ask, does it matter here in Jonah? Even if we believe God *could* miraculously sustain Jonah in a fish, is this story meant to be taken as historical? Does it make any difference whether a fish actually swallowed Jonah? Don't we get the basic point of the book—don't run away from God, or something like that—whether it really happened or not?

A Prophetic Sign

In the Bible, miracles don't appear in order to make a story more entertaining. They're signs that often have a prophetic purpose. They point to God's saving work and show his superiority over the idols people worship (Exod. 7–12; 1 Sam. 5:1–5; 1 Kings 18:20–40).[2] In this book, God calls a prophet to bring his word to the gentiles, which is unprecedented. Likewise, as we've seen, Israel in Jonah's time had probably been led into idolatry by King Jeroboam (2 Kings 14:23–24). A miraculous sign of God's saving power would make sense in these circumstances.

But we also have a direct confirmation that this miracle was a prophetic sign. When the Pharisees ask Jesus to prove that God really sent him, he says:

> An evil and adulterous generation seeks for a sign, but no sign will be given to it except the sign of Jonah. For just as Jonah was three days and three nights in the belly of the great fish, so will the Son of Man be three days and three nights in the heart of the earth. (Matt. 12:39–40)

When God sent a fish to swallow Jonah, Jesus says, he gave the world a sign. It pointed to the greatest miracle God has ever performed: "so will the Son of Man be three days and three nights in the heart of the earth." Jesus going down into the grave and rising after three days would be the sign that proved he was the Son of God, the Savior of the world, the one "greater than Jonah" (Matt. 12:41).

Jonah is thrown overboard because he clings to his sin. Jesus went down to death because we cling to ours. Jesus went down into the depths of death for us, but death had no claim on him. He had no sin. He stilled the storm of judgment so that we, too, can one day rise again.

Questions for Reflection

1. Do you think that doubting the historicity of Jonah's survival in the fish could affect our understanding of the meaning of this book? Why or why not?

---

[2] "Miracles," in *The Baker Illustrated Bible Dictionary*, ed. Tremper Longman III (Grand Rapids, MI: Baker Publishing Group, 2013), 1159–1160.

2 . What do you think Jesus means by "the sign of Jonah"?

Read Jonah 2:1–3; Matthew 27:45–50

Crying Out from the Abyss

Finally, Jonah responds to God. As far from God's presence as he could be, in the belly of the fish, he prays. His prayer is a poem, and it takes up almost a quarter of the book of Jonah.

I bet at some point you've felt distant from God. Most people have felt that way. Yet, as we've seen in chapter 1 of Jonah, in one sense it's impossible to be distant from God. He's everywhere. That's why Jonah's attempt to run from God was so ironic. He told the sailors that he feared the God "who made the sea and the dry land" (Jon. 1:9), yet he was on the sea trying to flee.

In another sense, though, every step Jonah has taken in this story has been away from God.

Sometimes it's not until we've reached complete desperation that we call out to God. Maybe you've been in a place like that. Maybe that's where you are now. You don't doubt that God is omnipresent, but you think, *He's far from me.* You think you should pray, but then you think, *How could I pray?* Your shame is too powerful. You know you've been moving away from God. You think, *Maybe I should just die.*

God is everywhere, but our sins keep us far from him: "Behold, the Lord's hand is not shortened, that it cannot save, or his ear dull, that it cannot hear; but your iniquities have made a separation between you and God" (Isa. 59:1–2). Have you ever felt like God didn't hear your prayers? Have you ever felt like God has turned his back on you because of your sin?

Here, in the fish, Jonah prays to God for the first time in this book. The pagan sailors prayed to the Lord, but Jonah stayed silent as he was cast into the ocean (Jon. 1:15–16). Only now, on the brink of death, does he cry out to God: "I called out to the Lord, out of my distress, and he answered me; out of the belly of Sheol I cried, and you heard my voice" (Jon. 2:2). Jonah has, essentially, just committed suicide. He chose to die rather than call out to God. But now, from the most forsaken place, he calls to God, and God answers him.

What does he mean by *Sheol*? It's the word the Jews used to describe the underworld. It basically means the grave (Ps. 6:5; Prov. 5:5). Jonah is saying, *I was in death's belly. I was in the land of the dead.* There's no place higher than God on his heavenly throne. But Jonah is in the lowest place. That's why he says, "For you cast me into the deep," and "all your waves and your billows passed over me" (Jon. 2:3). He's as far from God as he can possibly be.

He's as far down as he can go.

Waters of Judgment

The waters symbolize God's judgment. Jonah says "the flood surrounded me" (Jon. 2:3). A flood, of course, was God's first great act of judgment against humanity (Gen. 6:11–14). God provided Noah with an ark—but Jonah is submerged. When God led his people out of Egypt, he drowned Pharoah's army in the waters of the Red Sea (Exod. 14:27–28). Jonah, here, drowns in the waters of wrath—like the enemies of God.

The waters of baptism also represent judgment. The apostle Paul says, "Do you not know that all of us who have been baptized into Christ Jesus were baptized into his death? We were buried therefore with him by baptism into death, in order that, just as Christ was raised from the dead by the glory of the Father, we too might walk in newness of life" (Rom. 6:3–4). Jesus, who referred to his coming death and resurrection as the "sign of Jonah," endured our judgment on the cross. It's his baptism (Luke 12:50). When we're united to him by faith, we pass through those waters of judgment and come out of them into safety.

Will God Listen to You?

Do you think God hears your prayers when you're low? What if it's your fault that you're low? What if it's because of your sin? Like Jonah, you chose to run from God. Will God listen to you? When Jonah calls out to God, on the brink of death, under the waters of judgment, his prayer ascends all the way to God's throne.

Call out to God and he'll hear you. Why? Because when Jesus called to his Father from the cross, he received no answer. Jesus cried, "My God, my God, why have you forsaken me?" (Matt. 27:46). But he was left to drown.

God doesn't answer you because you're worthy. He answers because his Son bore your judgment. Because Jesus was forsaken for you. Because his cry wasn't heard.

Questions for Reflection

1. What's the relationship of Christ's crucifixion to baptism?

2. How does this story give you hope that God will hear you when you call to him in faith, regardless of what you've done?

Read Jonah 2:4; 1 Kings 8:44–52

What Is Jonah's Hope?

Sometimes to get the ear of important people, you need to be an important person yourself. Imagine trying to get a sit-down with the president of the United States. How easy would it be to get him to schedule a lunch with you so you could tell him what you think about the direction of the country? Not that easy, right? A lot of people want time with the president.

One particular group who may want the president's attention is prisoners because the president can pardon anyone he wants to. He can just say, "Hey, I want that guy out of prison," and—boom—he's out of prison. But if you want a presidential pardon, you need to have connections to the president. It's all about who you know, right?

When he was leaving office, Bill Clinton created a stir with his pardons. He pardoned someone serving a 15-year sentence for conspiracy to sell drugs. How did that person get the ear of the president? His father was a powerful leader in Los Angeles who'd made large donations to the president's political party. President Clinton also pardoned his half-brother, Roger Clinton, who'd been convicted of cocaine possession. Although he'd plead guilty to the charges, he was released from jail and his slate was wiped clean. He didn't have a criminal record anymore.

Here's what's so amazing about God, who's infinitely higher than any president. He listens to the voice of the one who is in prison, even when that person has directly offended him. Jonah isn't God's half-brother. He doesn't know a guy who knows a guy who once did God a favor. He can't appeal to what he's done or his connections to get the ear of God. On the contrary, everything that Jonah has done has only made him more and more distant from God.

And yet when Jonah prays—when he cries out for pardon—God hears him.

The Safe Zone

Why do you think God listens to Jonah's prayer? What would you say to someone who asked you this question? Would you say, "Well, God is gracious. That's just how he is." That's true. But the answer is hinted at in verse 4: "Then I said, 'I am driven away from your sight; yet I shall look again on your holy temple." While Jonah is fading away, almost dead, he brings to mind the temple of God. And there's a glimmer of hope.

Did you ever play tag when you were a kid? You get a group of friends together and you choose one of them to be *it*. The kid who's *it* has to chase around the other kids and when he tags another player, then that kid is *it*. Before the game starts, you identify a safe zone. Maybe it's the slide on the playground or the sandbox. It's the place where the guy who's *it* can't get you. It's the place where you're safe.

Do you know where the safe zone was for Israelites in Jonah's day? The temple of the Lord. God promised to dwell there among his people. It was the place where he would meet with them, where they could be in his presence. On the day when this temple was dedicated to the Lord, King Solomon prayed:

Yet have regard to the prayer of your servant and to his plea. O Lord my God, listening to the cry and to the prayer that your servant prays before you this day, that your eyes may be open night and day toward this house, the place of which you have said, 'My name shall be there,' that you may listen to the prayer that your servant offers toward this place. And listen to the plea of your servant and of your people Israel, when they pray toward this place. And listen in heaven your dwelling place, and when you hear, forgive. (1 Kings 8:28–30)

Later in the prayer, Solomon asks God to hear his people no matter how far away from the temple they are (1 Kings 8:44–52).

Jonah knows he's far from God, but he remembers the Lord. He says, *I will again look to the temple of the Lord, the place where God has promised to dwell, where his name and presence reside.* In the temple, priests made sacrifices for the people to make atonement for their sin. It's the place where those who are distant from God can look and find God's presence. They might be as low as *Sheol*, but when they lift their eyes to the temple of the Lord, where God has said, "I am here," their prayer, as Solomon asked, ascends all the way up to heaven.

Questions for Reflection

1. Why does Jonah say he'll "again look upon your holy temple"? What significance do you think the temple had for him?

2. All of us have some kind of "safe zone." We all see something as a refuge or fortress that can protect us when we're threatened. Is God the safe zone that you instinctively look to, or do you often look first to other things for security? If so, what are some of those things?

Notes

"AND THE LORD SPOKE TO THE FISH,

AND IT VOMITED JONAH OUT UPON THE

DRY LAND."

_____

Jonah 2:10

God *Saves* His Prophet

Read Jonah 2:5–6; Psalm 32:1–5

Repentant at Last?

From the depths, Jonah finally cries out to God. And God answers him. But we still may wonder why, exactly, Jonah calls out to God. It seemed like Jonah wanted to die, or at least had resigned himself to death. He asked the sailors to throw him overboard. What changed? Is it just that fear overwhelmed him when he finally faced death?

That seems likely. His prayer focuses on frightening imagery:

> The waters closed in over me to take my life;
> the deep surrounded me;
> weeds were wrapped about my head
> at the roots of the mountains.
> I went down to the land
> whose bars closed upon me forever. (Jon. 2:5–6)

Facing the terror of immanent death, Jonah has a change of heart. As far as we can tell, it's the fear of death that finally causes Jonah to relent and submit to God.

But, again, what Jonah *doesn't* say may be just as important. His prayer sounds very pious, and there's no reason to doubt his sincerity. He also sounded pious, though, on board the ship, when he told the sailors who he was: "I am a Hebrew, and I fear the Lord" (Jon. 1:9). Most likely, he said that sincerely. But what was he sincere *about*? He sincerely cherishes his Hebrew identity, and to be a Hebrew is to be one who fears the Lord. So, he told them who he sincerely believed he was.

His *actions*, though, showed no fear of the Lord.

Jonah has given us good reason to be suspicious about him. His prayer here, when we think about it, raises some questions. It's a song of thanksgiving. It follows a particular pattern found in the biblical psalms. It includes "(1) an introduction that attests that his prayer for deliverance was answered (v. 3), (2) a recounting of the crisis and of his deliverance from it (vv. 4–8), and (3) a subsequent vow to worship God for that deliverance (vv. 9–10)."[1] At first glance, it makes sense that Jonah would pray this kind of prayer in his circumstances.

But this form doesn't acknowledge why Jonah needs to be rescued. Jonah isn't in the fish because he was just in the wrong place at the wrong time. He didn't innocently misread the weather forecast. If a teenager calls home and tells her parents the car is totaled but, thankfully, she survived the crash without a scratch, two very different conversations might follow. If the accident happened because some bozo looking at his phone ran a red light, that's one thing. Her parents will probably feel angry at the other driver, but they'll be deeply relieved and thankful that their daughter's okay.

But if the accident happened because the teenager snuck out of the house, went to a party, drank six beers, and then tried to drive home, that's a different conversation. They'll still be relieved she's okay, but there's a serious reckoning coming. The cause of the accident changes the situation.

Jonah's story unfolds as a result of his rejection of God's calling for him to *go*. Jonah's sin and

---

[1] Timmer, *Gracious and Compassionate God*, 81.

rebellion have caused this disaster. Does he acknowledge this? Does Jonah feel shame or guilt? We're expecting a transformation of his character. Is that what we find?

In other words, is Jonah repentant at last?

Commentators disagree. Clearly, though, Jonah never directly refers to his sin. He says to God, "For you cast me into the deep," (Jon. 2:3) but he doesn't acknowledge the reason for this. He's terrified, it seems, but he never says he's sorry. He doesn't ask for forgiveness. One commentator says that "in psalms when sin is recognized as the cause of a writer's duress, he makes that element primary and seeks deliverance from sin before anything else (as in Ps. 32)."[2] That's not what Jonah does here. He's thankful to God, but he doesn't seem to acknowledge the cause of his plight.

Another commentator writes, "Is it not strange that Jonah expresses his eagerness to return to the temple, especially when there is no mention of his repentance or willingness to go to Nineveh?. . . .Is he counting on divine *hesed* to overlook his disobedience and cancel his commission?"[3] *Hesed* is the Hebrew word translated here as "steadfast love." It's God's covenant love. Might Jonah think that because he's a Hebrew, one of God's covenant people, God will receive him back without repentance and obedience?

Questions for Reflection

1. Describe a psalm of thanksgiving. How might recognizing that Jonah's prayer follows this form help us understand its meaning?

2. What is repentance?

---

[2] Timmer, *A Gracious and Compassionate God*, 81–82.

[3] James S. Ackerman, "Jonah," in *The Literary Guide to the Bible*, ed. Robert Alter and Frank Kermode (Cambridge, MA: Harvard University Press, 1997), 238.

Read Jonah 2:7–9; Psalm 51

Look to the Temple

The temple is the place of God's presence. It's the center of Israel's existence and identity. By evoking the temple here, for a second time in his prayer, Jonah expresses a hope of being once again in God's presence: "When my life was fainting away, I remembered the Lord, and my prayer came to you, into your holy temple" (Jon. 2:7). He's confident that God has heard him and will rescue him.

When you feel distant from God—when you feel like you're in the valley of death—and you question God's goodness and mercy, what do you need to do? You need to look to the place where God has promised to reside. You need to look to the temple of God.

The temple of God for us, though, isn't a place. It's a person. The temple Jonah looked to was meant to point us to a greater temple, an even greater dwelling of God among men, where an even greater sacrifice for sins would take place: Jesus's body.

In Jesus's time, people used the temple in Jerusalem for many things other than prayer and sacrifices. At one point in his ministry, Jesus went to the temple and chased out the merchants and money-changers with a whip:

> And he poured out the coins of the money-changers and overturned their tables. And he told those who sold pigeons, "Take these things away; do not make my Father's house a house of trade." . . . The Jews watching him asked, "What sign do you show us for doing these things?" Jesus answered them, "Destroy this temple, and in three days I will raise it up." The Jews then said, "It has taken forty-six years to build this temple, and you will raise it up in three days?" But he was speaking about the temple of his body. When therefore he was raised from the dead, his disciples remembered that he had said this, and they believed the Scripture and the word that Jesus had spoken. (John 2:15–22)

When asked for a sign of his authority to purify the temple, Jesus says that his resurrection will be the only sign—he also says this when he tells the Pharisees that the "sign of Jonah" will prove his identity.

But he also redefines the temple. The temple that will be destroyed and then raised is his body. That's where God's presence dwells now. That's where salvation and life can be found. When we look to Jesus Christ, we see the true and final way of entering God's presence.

Jonah: Pharisee or Tax Collector?

Jonah's prayer reaches God. Yet the next thing he says may remind us of a parable Jesus tells about two men praying in the temple. One offers a prayer of thanksgiving, the other a prayer of repentance:

> He also told this parable to some who trusted in themselves that they were righteous, and treated others with contempt: "Two men went up into the temple to pray, one a Pharisee and the other a tax collector. The Pharisee, standing by himself, prayed thus: 'God, I thank you that I am not like other men, extortioners, unjust, adulterers, or even like this tax collector. I fast twice a week; I give tithes of all that I get.' But the tax collector, standing far off, would not even lift up his eyes to heaven, but beat his breast, saying, 'God, be merciful to

me, a sinner!' I tell you, this man went down to his house justified, rather than the other. For everyone who exalts himself will be humbled, but the one who humbles himself will be exalted.'" (Luke 18:9–14)

Both men look to the temple. Both men go there to pray to God and be in his presence.

Here, Jonah says, "Those who pay regard to vain idols forsake their hope of steadfast love. But I with the voice of thanksgiving will sacrifice to you" (Jon. 2:8). This is true. This is orthodox belief. Idolators separate themselves from God's love.

But what does it mean coming from Jonah in this context? What does he mean by contrasting idolators and himself? Is this an acknowledgement of his sin, a confession that he has strayed from God? Is he admitting that he's been no better than pagan idolators, but has now turned back to God? Is this a form of repentance? Is Jonah like the tax collector?

Or is this the Jonah we've seen all along? Is this the Jonah who said, "I am a Hebrew, and I fear the Lord" (Jon. 1:9), the Jonah proud of his ethnic and religious heritage, determined to keep himself away from gentile idolators? Is he more like the Pharisee in Jesus's parable: "God, I thank you that I am not like other men, extortioners, unjust, adulterers, or even like this tax collector. I fast twice a week; I give tithes of all that I get" (Luke 18:11–12)?

Given the fact that he makes no clear reference to his guilt in this psalm, we may not want to give him the benefit of the doubt.

Which Kind of Sacrifice?

Jonah vows that he, like the gentile sailors, will make a sacrifice to God. Of course, he doesn't know what's transpired up on the surface, but he says, "I with the voice of thanksgiving will sacrifice to you; what I have vowed I will pay" (Jon. 2:9).

When we see Jesus drive the merchants from the temple, we're reminded that it's a holy place. God's presence is dangerous. To approach God, we must be holy. The temple isn't a place to hang out and do whatever you want. That's why the Old Testament has so many rules about worship. And that's why God appointed priests to make sacrifices to atone for the people's sin. Only in this way could they come near to God safely.

God's law described many different sacrifices, but there are two main kinds—thanksgiving and guilt. Through sacrifices of thanksgiving, God's people brought a tribute to their king. It showed their love and gratitude toward him. But these sacrifices didn't atone for sin. That wasn't their purpose.

Jonah says he'll sacrifice with "a voice of thanksgiving." Even as he says he'll sacrifice, he doesn't acknowledge any need for atonement. Just as a psalm of thanksgiving praises God for saving someone from danger but not necessarily sin, this sacrifice of thanksgiving can offer praise to God without reference to guilt.

Therefore, as we reach the triumphant, final note of this song, how should we read it? Jonah says, "Salvation belongs to the Lord!" (Jon. 2:9). Is this the joyful praise of a repentant sinner who knows he's been saved by grace alone? Or is it the pious and proud orthodoxy of a proto-Pharisee?

Again, commentators disagree. And the story isn't over yet. Will Jonah be a different man when he returns to the land of the living? Will he do God's will with joy and humility? We'll find out.

We can know, though, that the one "greater than Jonah" (Matt. 12:41) has come. He's the temple.

He's also the priest. And he's the sacrifice:

> And every priest stands daily at his service, offering repeatedly the same sacrifices, which can never take away sins. But when Christ had offered for all time a single sacrifice for sins, he sat down at the right hand of God, waiting from that time until his enemies should be made a footstool for his feet. For by a single offering he has perfected for all time those who are being sanctified. (Heb. 10:11–14)

Maybe you feel distant from him right now. Maybe you're distant because of sins you choose to commit. Maybe you feel like you're in a pit you can't escape from. You may not feel God's presence, but God has told you where you can find him. He says, *Look toward the temple.*

Let's direct our eyes to the true temple of God, Jesus Christ, and in faith, call out to him, even from the belly of *Sheol*. When our prayers rise to him, he will lift us up. You may not feel immediate relief. You may not even feel better. Your problems may not disappear. But he's promised he will lift us up from the grave. Our lives may not end in prosperity and peace, but we can be sure—through Christ—that we will live forever, in the light of God's presence.

Questions for Reflection

1. What's the relationship between Jesus and the temple in Jerusalem?

2. What are the two main kinds of sacrifice? What does each one mean? What does each type of sacrifice say about how we come into the presence of God?

Read Jonah 2:10; Genesis 1:3

Jonah is Saved

Jonah's prayer is over. Our third-person narrator returns. God responds to Jonah's words by speaking to the fish, who returns Jonah safely to dry land. Jonah is saved.

Does this action speak for itself? Is it self-evident that Jonah's prayer has pleased God? Do we know God's reasons for rescuing Jonah?

God spoke to the fish, but the narrator doesn't record God's words: "And the Lord spoke to the fish" (Jon. 2:10). We haven't heard God's words since he called Jonah at the beginning of the book (Jon. 1:2). Yet he's controlled the story. He's revealed his will in other ways. He sent a storm after Jonah. He called the wind and the waves into his service. He made himself known to the sailors through Jonah and brought them into submission. He called the fish to swallow Jonah. And now, the focus of his attention, Jonah, has bowed to his will as well.

These first two chapters show God's omnipresence and sovereign power. He uses his creatures to make known—and accomplish—what pleases him.

Raised by God's Word

What matters here in verse 10 isn't what God said but that he spoke. As in the beginning, when God created the heavens and the earth, his word fulfills his purpose (Gen. 1). And since Jesus tells us that Jonah's return to land is a picture of his resurrection, we're reminded that God will also one day raise us up from death by his word:

> That we may then, without hesitation and doubt, be convinced of the restoration which God promises to us, let us remember that the world was by him created out of nothing by his word and bidding, and is still thus sustained. But if this general truth is not sufficient, let this history of Jonah come to our minds, — that God commanded a fish to cast forth Jonah: for how was it that Jonah escaped safe and was delivered? Even because it so pleased God, because the Lord commanded; and this word at this day retains the same efficacy. By that power then, by which he works all things, we also shall one day be raised up from the dead.[4]

As God's word accomplishes his purpose in Jonah's "resurrection," so it will one day in ours.

A clue, though, that might tell us something about God's thoughts as the first half of the book of Jonah comes to an end is the verb "vomited." The fish vomits Jonah out—like a sickness or a bad piece of crab meat. Vomit is no more appealing to the biblical authors than it is to us. In the Old Testament, it's associated at times with judgment.[5] In Leviticus 18:25–28, God tells Israel that the promised land "vomited out" those who lived there before Israel because of their sin, and Israel, too, will be vomited out of the land if they disobey God. The Assyrians, of course, conquer Israel not long after Jonah and remove God's people from the promised land. It's possible the author uses this verb so that we'll make that connection.

Vomit can also be associated with humiliation.[6] Referring to God's judgment on Moab, one of Israel's enemies, God says, "Make him drunk, because he magnified himself against the Lord, so that Moab shall wallow in his vomit, and he too shall be held in derision" (Jer. 48:26). The image of Jonah as vomit may be intended to show his humiliation even in his deliverance. He, too, it seems, has "magnified himself against the Lord." He's defied God by refusing to obey his call. So far, this story seems to be showing that the gap between Israel and her pagan neighbors is not as great as Jonah thinks—if it even exists at all. This verb, vomit, then may reinforce Jonah's unworthiness.

Jesus compares his own death and resurrection to Jonah's experience (Matt. 12:38–42). As we've seen, though, both similarities and differences exist between Jonah and Jesus. Jesus, who died and entered the tomb because of his obedience to God's call, didn't get vomited out of the grave.

---

[4] John Calvin, *Commentary on Jonah, Micah, and Nahum*, trans. John Owen (Grand Rapids, MI: Christian Classics Ethereal Library), 80, https://ccel.org/ccel/calvin/calcom28/calcom28.iii.2.ix.html.

[5] Youngblood, *Jonah*, 114.

[6] Youngblood, *Jonah*, 114.

The apostle Peter, in his Pentecost sermon, says, "God raised him up, loosing the pangs of death, because it was not possible for him to be held by it" (Acts 2:24). The power of God raises Jesus and conquers death. It's God's greatest miracle, by which he overcomes the world and begins the new creation. It's the vindication of Jesus (Rom. 1:4), the sign he told those who asked for one to look for (Matt. 12:39).

But Jonah's ejection from the fish does not serve as vindication.

Jonah may be humiliated, but he's safe "upon the dry land" (Jon. 2:10). After going deeper into the depths with each turn of events, he's now risen up. His ordeal, it seems, is over. Enjoying a moment of relief, we wait to see what God, the ultimate author of the story, will do next. As we've seen, he can't be stopped.

Whatever else may be true of Jonah, he's still a prophet called by God.

Questions for Reflection

1. Why do you think the narrator says God spoke to the fish but doesn't tell us what he said? Should God's thoughts about Jonah's prayer be clear to us? Why or why not?

2. Does it seem significant that the text says that the fish "vomited" Jonah out? Are there good reasons to think this situation might echo other passages in the Old Testament that use this verb?

"THEN THE WORD OF THE LORD CAME TO

JONAH THE SECOND TIME."

Jonah 3:1

Again *in* God's Presence

Read Jonah 1:1–2, 3:1–2; Romans 5:6–8

God Calls Jonah

Our story, it seems, starts over. We know, of course, what Jonah has been through. We know a fish vomited Jonah out onto land. But it's as if he went through all that terror and agony only to end up where he started. He's confronted with the same call.

The second half of the story of Jonah begins with an almost perfect echo of Jonah 1:1–2: "Then the word of the Lord came to Jonah the second time, saying, 'Arise, go to Nineveh, that great city, and call out against it the message that I tell you" (Jon. 3:1–2).

We don't know where Jonah is. We only know that he's back on land, "restored to the realm of life and order."[1] Like the first call, nothing is described. This is the same sense of being outside space and time. Only the word of God matters.[2]

It's just Jonah confronted once again with the call of God.

As Jonah's response to the word of God led to all the action of the first half of the book, we now prepare for a new drama. Will God's message be delivered this time? If so, how? And how will the menacing Assyrians respond to God?

As this new act opens, all we know is that Jonah is alive, he is again in God's presence, and he has been given a second chance.

Do You Believe In Second Chances?

When people make big mistakes in life, should they be given another chance? You might say, "Well, it depends on what they've done. How bad was the mistake?" One of the most difficult things for us to do is give second chances. We want second chances for ourselves, but giving a second chance to someone who has hurt us is a different story.

Imagine you have a large amount of money. You give it to an asset manager who can invest it for you. But soon, you get a phone call. You discover that this manager spent all your money on Armani suits, sports cars, and trips to the Pacific Islands. Your money's gone. You call him to see if this is true. He says, "Yeah, sorry. All that money was just too tempting. But I know you'll forgive me because you're a Christian."

Would you give him a second chance? Would you say, "Yes, I'm going to trust you with my money again even though you've shown that you're not trustworthy"? Probably not. Giving second chances is difficult, especially when it involves something big. It's not like he just forgot to take out the trash.

But that's what God does here. It's like putting your money back in the hands of the money manager who swindled you.

Our God gives second chances. And God doesn't just give second chances, he orchestrates them.

---

1 Youngblood, *Jonah*, 123.
2 Youngblood, *Jonah*, 123.

He so desires to see his children repent that he paves the path for them.

Why Does God Give Jonah a Second Chance?

Why does God give Jonah a second chance? Why does he give anybody a second chance? Why does he go to such great lengths to give Jonah a second chance? Let's answer that through a process of elimination. What are *not* the reasons God gives Jonah a second chance?

It's not because his sins weren't a big deal. Sometimes, when people apologize to us, we say, "No big deal." It really didn't put us out that much. We appreciate their acknowledgment of fault and that's it. We're good. But even the sailors see that what Jonah did was a very big deal. They said, "What is this that you have done!" (Jon. 1:10). The apostle Paul says, "The wages of sin is death" (Rom. 6:23). That's what Jonah deserves.

God also doesn't give Jonah a second chance because he needs Jonah. In 2007, Michael Vick, a star quarterback, went to jail for 23 months for running an illegal dog-fighting ring. After he was released, he joined a new NFL team. He was too talented to be ignored. He got a second chance because a team needed him.

But God doesn't need anyone. John the Baptist said to the crowds in Israel, "And do not begin to say to yourselves, 'We have Abraham as our father.' For I tell you, God is able from these stones to raise up children for Abraham" (Luke 3:8). God doesn't need us and he didn't need Jonah. God can raise up prophets from the dust of the ground.

Most often, we'll only give second chances to someone who didn't really offend us or mess up anything important to us. And if we need something from someone, we might have to give him a second chance. But God gives a second chance to a man who had greatly offended him, who had failed in an important task, and whom God didn't need.

So why does God give Jonah a second chance?

Because God loves his people. Only love explains God's actions. Would you, if you're a parent, stop loving your children if they disobeyed you, destroyed the gifts you gave them, or rejected you? Would you refuse to forgive them if they came back to you? Wouldn't you do whatever you could to bring them back? Jonah is God's wayward child.

But human love—even parental love—isn't perfect. God's love is the "steadfast love" that Jonah referred to in his prayer (Jon. 2:8)—God's unshakable covenant love. No English term fully captures the meaning of the Hebrew word for this love, *hesed*. But this *hesed* love explains why God entrusts Jonah again with this great responsibility.

God Loves You

God doesn't love Jonah because Jonah is faithful. Jonah isn't lovable or good. Human love works that way, but not God's love. God shows the greatness of his love by loving a man who forfeited any right to be loved. God shows that his love is bigger than our failures. He loves us in spite of our weaknesses. He gives us second chances even though we're guilty.

And it's now, after receiving this love, that Jonah goes to the barbaric Assyrians with God's message.

God pursued you. Not because you're innocent. Not because your sin is a minor issue. Not because he doesn't care that you dropped the ball. Not because he needs you. God pursued you because he loves you.

Questions for Reflection

1. What's the most difficult thing you've ever had to forgive? Are there people who you still can't bring yourself to forgive? If so, why?

2. What does the Hebrew word *hesed* mean?

Read Jonah 1:3, 3:3

The Prophet Obeys

God's call sounds almost the same as it did in the beginning. But the prophet's response is polar opposite. Instead of fleeing west to Tarshish (Jon. 1:3), he goes east: "So Jonah arose and went to Nineveh" (Jon. 3:3). The narrator doesn't reveal Jonah's thoughts or desires. His direction of travel tells us, it seems, all we need to know.

Repentance means "turning back." When we repent, we turn from sin to Jesus. On the surface, Jonah's response to God is the perfect picture of repentance—a 180-degree turn. His first itinerary sent him in the direction opposite to the one God told him to travel; his new itinerary makes a beeline for Nineveh. The first route opposed God's will; the new route obeys it without question.

And now, the action unfolds. What will happen as a result of Jonah's new direction?

What We Already Know Will Happen

God's first call ended with Jonah in the belly of a fish. From there, Jonah cried out to God, and God delivered him from death. God *pursued* Jonah—set the created order against Jonah—so he could give Jonah a second chance.

God has been in control every step of the way. He "hurled a great wind upon the sea" to create the storm (Jon. 1:4). He caused the lot to fall on Jonah (Jon. 1:7). When the sailors wanted to save Jonah, God stirred up even more menacing waves (Jon. 1:13). He called the fish to swallow Jonah (Jon. 1:17) and then told it to spit him out (Jon. 2:10).

Jonah knows this. In the fish, he prayed, "For you cast me into the deep . . . all your waves and your billows passed over me" (Jon. 2:3). He knows God has controlled everything. He can't escape God's call.

So, Jonah knows—and we know—that God is going to fulfill his purpose.

Jonah goes to Nineveh "according to the word of the Lord" (Jon. 3:3). God's power and presence comes through his word. Jonah doesn't just have a message to pass along. He has an atomic bomb. He's bringing divine power into the great city.

And its terrifying force has nothing to do with the messenger's belief in the message. We know from the first half of Jonah that God's plan doesn't even depend on the prophet's willingness to go. We know God's plan will succeed.

Arrival in the Great City

God calls Nineveh "that great city" throughout the book of Jonah (Jon. 1:2, 3:2, 4:11). Here, when Jonah arrives in Nineveh, the narrator also calls it a "great city" (Jon. 1:4, 3:3). This repetition tells us that this description matters. Here, though, the English Standard Version of the Bible includes the word "exceedingly," as though the author wants to emphasize even more just how impressive this city is: "Now Nineveh was an exceedingly great city" (Jon. 3:3). Initially, this seems to make sense, since what follows describes Nineveh as "three days' journey in breadth." If so, it's an enormous city.

But is Nineveh's physical size the main issue? The phrase translated "exceedingly" is actually *elohim* with a preposition: literally, "to God." But what does "a great city to God" mean? Which god? It's been interpreted as "a great city to the gods" and "an important city to God."[3] Is the point that Nineveh was a pagan religious center in Assyria or that God has a special concern for it? Several commentators argue that the context of this phrase suggests the latter.[4] God cares for the great city as his own.

The phrase translated "three days' journey in breadth" probably doesn't refer to the literal size of the city. Commentators disagree, though, about its meaning. According to Bryan D. Estelle:

> The phrase is actually intended to indicate that the city is very far away when Jonah begins his journey of six hundred miles—much more than a literal three days' journey. The phrase is not meant, therefore, to describe the size of the city or the length of Jonah's stay; rather it is used figuratively and idiomatically to express the long distance Jonah would have to travel in order to arrive at Nineveh.[5]

If so, then we have a great city, far from the promised land of Israel—yet cared for by God.

Jonah, a model of repentance, arrives in the great pagan city, armed with the word of God. It took a near-death experience to get him on board with the mission, but now he's in the gentile city that God claims as his own.

---

[3] Youngblood, *Jonah*, 131.

[4] Youngblood, *Jonah*, 131; Estelle, *Salvation through Judgment and Mercy*, 107–108; Timmer, *A Gracious and Compassionate God*, 95.

[5] Estelle, *Salvation through Judgment and Mercy*, 108.

Questions for Reflection

1. How important is Jonah's obedience to the ultimate outcome of the story? How do his will and God's will interact?

2. Why do you think Nineveh continues to be called the "great city" in this story?

Read Jonah 3:4; Psalm 7:12–13; Ezekiel 18:32

The Message

In 2004, around Christmas time, a tsunami struck southeast Asia, killing 200,000 people. Here's what was especially tragic: many people knew the tsunami was coming. But they couldn't warn villagers living in remote areas. They couldn't get the message to them.

Warnings, if they're heeded, can save lives. But if the message is never heard, the results are devastating.

God sends Jonah to warn Nineveh of the tsunami of God's judgment. But Jonah doesn't want those in danger to hear. He probably thinks they're so bad they don't deserve God's forgiveness. At least, it seems, that's been true until now.

God's justice is severe (Psalm 7:12–13). It's flawless. It's matched only by his love, patience, and mercy (Ezek. 18:32). In chapter 2, we saw the love of God extended to Jonah. Now, it comes to Nineveh.

Jonah comes into the city and says, "Yet forty days, and Nineveh shall be overthrown!" (Jon. 3:4). This is God's message of judgment—and mercy.

Why Should Nineveh Believe Jonah?

Getting the warning out there is one thing. But getting people to believe the warning is something else. It's not very easy.

Imagine you're walking out of church one Sunday. As you approach your car, you see a man who looks like he has just walked 500 miles, wearing a long, unkempt beard and ragged clothes. He's crying out in a loud voice, from the middle of the parking lot, "Forty days until this city is overthrown!"

Would you believe him? Probably not. So why should Nineveh believe Jonah?

During Jonah's time, the Assyrian Empire had declined from the height of its power. Powerful regional officials threatened its political unity.[6] Daniel C. Timmer writes, "In addition to this instability at the level of government, a number of famines, revolts and plagues are recorded in Assyrian records, events whose evil portent was believed to be clearly indicated by accompanying eclipses."[7] Bad omens from both politics and nature came one after another. The Assyrians, like the sailors, probably assumed the gods were angry.

If a disheveled prophet shows up in the church parking lot in a time of economic prosperity, you might hear the message of doom and think, *This guy's crazy.* But if there's already famine, revolts, and signs in the heavens, maybe he'll seem a little more believable. Could it be that God had prepared Nineveh to hear Jonah's message?

The power of God's word doesn't depend on his general providential work in nature. But both eclipses and prophecies come from God. He uses both, together, in whatever way he chooses. It's likely that he primed the Ninevites for Jonah's arrival. As we'll see, though, what matters to the author of the book of Jonah is the work of the word.[8]

Why 40 Days?

Jonah has brought a message of destruction. But it also tells them about God's mercy. Jonah doesn't say, "You have 40 minutes to live." Nineveh has 40 days to amend its ways.

Why 40 days? The Bible often uses the number 40 for times of testing or trial. In the flood, it rained for 40 days (Gen. 7:4). The children of Israel wandered in the wilderness for 40 years (Num. 14:34). Jesus fasted in the desert 40 days, enduring temptation (Mark 1:13). God gives Nineveh 40 days because although God is just and holy, he cares about sinners. The apostle Peter says that God is "patient toward you, not wishing that any should perish, but that all should reach repentance" (2 Peter 3:9).

God has made known his coming wrath, but he has given Nineveh time to repent. Like a warning about a coming tsunami, it's a message of mercy.

But Why Is God So Judgmental?

Maybe, though, it's not God's mercy that makes an impression on you here. Instead, maybe you're offended by the idea that God punishes sin. Maybe you think, *I believe in a God of love, not a God of wrath.* The destruction God announces, you may think, isn't loving. *Why doesn't God just let people do what they want?*

In 2016, gunmen entered the offices of *Charlie Hedbo*, a French satirical magazine, and began shooting. As they murdered people, they cried, "God is great!" Whether you're religious or not, when

---

[6] Timmer, *A Gracious and Compassionate God*, 92.

[7] Timmer, *A Gracious and Compassionate God*, 94.

[8] Youngblood, *Jonah*, 135.

you hear stories like this you feel anger and a longing for justice. Can you imagine how intense these feelings would be if your friends and family members were killed in that office?

Imagine if these men, instead of being punished, received a pardon. Imagine the authorities saying, "What you did was evil, but we're going to let you return to society. Just promise you won't do it again." How would you feel about that? How do you think people would respond? They'd probably cry out against the government. They'd think the legal system was corrupt. They'd say, "You want to forgive these monsters? They should face the consequences. They should get what they deserve."

Don't we rightly feel angry when murderers or white-collar crooks or war criminals get off scot-free?

It's not loving to allow sin to run wild. The judge who lets the murderer go free isn't loving to the family of the victims or to those he might kill in the future. Many of us have experienced injustices. Our hearts yearn for retribution, for justice, for good to prevail. A good God won't allow darkness to overcome light. He won't allow injustice to win or hatred to destroy love.

God judges the injustices in the world—but he gives us time to repent.

The Offense of Forgiveness

How can God do this and still be a just God? If the Ninevites heed the warning and repent, how will justice be done? Think of the tens of thousands they've slaughtered or enslaved. How can God pass over this?

We may be offended by God's judgment, but we can be offended even more by forgiveness. C.S. Lewis writes:

> Everyone says forgiveness is a lovely idea, until they have something to forgive, as we had during the war (World War II). And then, to mention the subject at all is to be greeted with howls of anger. It is not that people think this too high and difficult a virtue: it is that they think it hateful and contemptible. "That sort of talk makes me sick," they say. And half of you already want to ask me, "I wonder how you'd feel about forgiving the Gestapo if you were a Pole or a Jew?"

How can God forgive without insulting the victims of sin?

The God who loved you enough to pursue you loved you enough to take upon himself the guilt and shame of your sin. When Jonah goes down into the waters, it's a sign of judgment and death.

When he's vomited out, it's a sign of resurrection. Jonah, like you and me, is a sinner who deserved to die. But Jonah points to Jesus, who endured a death he didn't deserve because he loved us.

In Jesus, justice has been done. In Jesus, we can be free from judgment. In Jesus, we are free to forgive.

We, like Jonah, went into the waters of baptism and died. We died with Christ (Gal. 2:20). We ascended out of the waters by faith, with new life. We were given a second chance, an opportunity that, going forward, we can't mess up. It's not a three-strikes-and-you're-out policy. It's freedom from judgment and it can't be lost. Justice has been done, completely and forever, on the cross.

Questions for Reflection

1. Do you see Jonah's message to Nineveh as merciful? Why or why not?

2. How do you think God's word and his general providential rule over creation relate to each other?

"WHEN GOD SAW WHAT THEY DID, HOW

THEY TURNED FROM THEIR EVIL WAY,

GOD RELENTED OF THE DISASTER THAT

HE HAD SAID HE WOULD DO TO THEM,

AND HE DID NOT DO IT."

_____

Jonah 3:10

God *and* *the* Great City

Read Jonah 3:5–8; Revelation 20:11–15

Nineveh Calls Out to God

"No prophet within the biblical tradition has ever had such success. Jonah flees his divine commission, and the entire crew ends up worshiping YHWH. He speaks five words in Nineveh, and the whole city instantly turns away from its 'evil.'"[1]

Jonah proclaimed God's message in Nineveh: "Yet forty days, and Nineveh shall be overthrown!" (Jon. 3:4). Five Hebrew words. This may be the full message God gave Jonah. It could also be a summary of what Jonah preached.[2]

But it might be that Jonah has abridged God's message. It's notable that Jonah's words in the biblical text don't say who sent him, the reason for this judgment, or what—if anything—the Ninevites can do to avoid destruction. The latter two items are, according to Kevin J. Youngblood, "typical features of doom oracles against a foreign nation."[3] He continues, "These omissions raise the suspicions that Jonah's obedience is not all that it appears to be and that he may not have repeated the divine message exactly as he received it."[4] Maybe Jonah's 180-degree turn isn't what it seemed. Maybe the repentance his obedience suggested didn't go very far beneath the surface.

But it doesn't matter, at least in terms of the power of the message. With five words, he brings the great city to its knees.

Then he disappears from the scene.[5]

The Word in the City

Nineveh hears the word of God, and "the people of Nineveh believed God" (Jon. 3:5). As far as we know, Jonah didn't mention God. But it doesn't say they believed Jonah. They've heard God's word, so they're dealing with God.

The Ninevites' response may allude to Abraham: "And he believed the Lord, and he counted it to him as righteousness" (Gen. 15:6). When the word of God came to Abraham, he was a gentile. He wasn't circumcised. In fact, Israel didn't exist yet. God, at the time he called Abraham, dealt with the human race as a whole.[6] But Abraham heard God's word and responded with faith.

And God said that Abraham, as we've seen, would be a blessing to the whole world (Gen. 12:3). Nineveh's response of trust in what God says reminds us of God's plan for the human race.[7]

From verse 5 through the end of the chapter, Jonah is offstage. This scene belongs to Nineveh and the word of God. In verse 5, the word is the subject of the sentence: "The word reached the King of Nineveh, and he arose from his throne, removed his robe, covered himself with sackcloth, and sat

---

[1] Ackerman, "Jonah," 239–240.

[2] Timmer, *A Gracious and Compassionate God*, 96.

[3] Youngblood, *Jonah*, 133.

[4] Youngblood, *Jonah*, 133.

[5] Youngblood, *Jonah*, 135.

[6] Youngblood, *Jonah*, 135.

[7] Youngblood, *Jonah*, 135.

in ashes." The word—not Jonah—reaches the pagan king and humbles him to the dust.

This resembles Martin Luther's summary of the Bible's role in the 16th-century Reformation: "I simply taught, preached, and wrote God's Word; otherwise I did nothing. And while I slept, or drank Wittenberg beer with my friends Philip and Amsdorf, the Word so greatly weakened the papacy that no prince or emperor ever inflicted such losses upon it. I did nothing; the Word did everything."[8] Luther's motives likely differed from Jonah's, but in both situations, it's the word that brings down the great. It doesn't depend on the messenger; the word has a life of its own.

The Great City Calls Out to God

Chapter 1 ended with the sailors calling out to God (Jon. 1:14). In chapter 2, Jonah calls out to God (Jon. 2:1). Now, the king of Nineveh's decree says of every beast and human being in the city, "let them call out mightily to God" (Jon. 3:8).

How should we understand this response of Nineveh to God's message? They seem, like the sailors, highly sympathetic. They immediately and comprehensively humble themselves before God—from the king all the way down to the animals (Jon. 3:8). Bryan D. Estelle says, "it was total repentance."[9] According to John H. Walton, though, "evidence for a conversion to true Yahwism is difficult to find in the text. Unquestionably, they repent of 'their evil ways.' But there is no mention of turning to Yahweh, being instructed about the covenant, or discarding their other gods."[10] Timmer concludes that Nineveh's repentance was "partial and incomplete."[11]

This is clearly a remarkable repentance of some kind. But is it merely a temporary response to a particular coming judgment, or is it an inner transformation and a lasting allegiance to God? We may not be able to come to a final answer about the inner state of the Assyrians. And maybe we're not supposed to. We do know that any national allegiance to God didn't last (2 Kings 17:24–33).

Estelle points out, though, two functions of Nineveh's repentance that are vital to the book's message. First, Nineveh's immediate response to God's word differs dramatically from Jonah's. It wasn't until his last breath that Jonah submitted to God. Second, "since Jonah represents Israel, the author has used Nineveh as a foil to indict Israel indirectly for her own lack of repentance."[12] The prophet Amos, who lived at the same time as Jonah, writes:

> Then the Lord said,
> "Behold, I am setting a plumb line
> in the midst of my people Israel;
> I will never again pass by them;
> the high places of Isaac shall be made desolate,
> and the sanctuaries of Israel shall be laid waste,
> and I will rise against the house of
> Jeroboam with the sword." (Amos 7:8–9)

The message of judgment is as much for Israel as it is for Assyria.

---

[8] Quoted in Carl R. Trueman, *Luther on the Christian Life* (Wheaton, IL: Crossway, 2015), 94–95.

[9] Estelle, *Salvation through Judgment and Mercy*, 110.

[10] John H. Walton, "Jonah," in *Theological Interpretation of the Old Testament: A Book-by-Book Summary*, ed. Kevin J. Vanhoozer (Grand Rapids, MI: Baker, 2008), 271.

[11] Timmer, *A Gracious and Compassionate God*, 104.

[12] Estelle, *Salvation through Judgment and Mercy*, 110.

Also, unlike both the sailors and Jonah, the king's proclamation clearly acknowledges the sin that has brought judgment: "Let everyone turn from his evil way and from the violence that is in his hands" (Jon. 3:8). This repentance looks more like the repentance of the tax collector in Jesus's parable (Luke 18:12–14) than Jonah's did.

Who Is Called to Repent?

Sin isn't a Ninevite problem. It's a human problem. The same judgment that threatened Nineveh threatens Israel. And this same judgment threatens you and me.

Do you believe God about the coming judgment that will overthrow the world? The apostle Paul told the Greeks, "The times of ignorance God overlooked, but now he commands all people everywhere to repent, because he has fixed a day on which he will judge the world in righteousness by a man whom he has appointed; and of this he has given assurance to all by raising him from the dead" (Acts 17:30–31). God has fixed the day, and the clock is ticking.

When God says these things, do you believe him? Let God's message to Nineveh serve as a warning for us. Even today, his warnings are a sign of his grace. They're a call to repentance.

Jesus is the judge. The resurrection that assures that he is the Son of God also assures us that he'll return in judgment. But if we, by faith, repent of our sins and place our trust in his cross—where God executed his justice—the day of his return will be one of unimaginable light and peace.

Questions for Reflection

1.   What do you think Martin Luther meant when he said, "I did nothing; the Word did everything"?

2.   Jonah is "off-screen" in this scene. Do you think we're supposed to forget about him—at least temporarily? Or should we still be thinking about him as we see Nineveh respond to God's word?

Read Jonah 3:9; Acts 17:16–29

The Unknown God

When the apostle Paul went to Greece with the message of salvation in Christ, he said, "Men of Athens, I perceive that in every way you are very religious. For as I passed along and observed the objects of your worship, I found also an altar with this inscription: 'To the unknown god.' What therefore you worship as unknown, this I proclaim to you" (Acts 17:22–23).

Like Paul, Jonah was called to bring the knowledge of God to the gentiles. But on the ship, Jonah stayed silent until he was forced to speak when the lots revealed his guilt. The sailors had rushed around the deck of the ship in anguish because they didn't know the God who caused the storm. Jonah finally made him known when the circumstances God had arranged left him no choice.

Now, Jonah has obediently gone to Nineveh. He proclaims God's word of judgment. This results in the seemingly instantaneous repentance of the whole city. God's word has come to them in power.

But we still might wonder about the message. Jonah doesn't mention God at all, much less describe him in detail—at least from what we see in the text. It could be that the author has summarized Jonah's message. But what else did Jonah say? If it's a summary, should we expect that Jonah's five-word message of doom is still basically the gist of it?

Comparing Jonah's message to Paul's elaborate effort to make God known to the Athenians at least prompts the question: even as they respond so dramatically to God's word, what do the Ninevites know about the God they're dealing with?

Who Knows?

The king of Nineveh sets aside the symbols of his power—his throne and royal robes—when the word of God comes to him. Then he "covered himself with sackcloth and sat in ashes" (Jon. 3:6). These are symbols of mourning that show his repentance. He then tells his whole city to fast and repent (Jon. 3:7–8). These seem to be fitting responses to the word of God.

Then he says, "Who knows? God may turn and relent and turn from his fierce anger, so that we may not perish" (Jon. 3:9). According to Youngblood, this question "who knows?" appears in several other Old Testament passages and suggests an affirmation of "divine freedom and, therefore, the uncertainty of outcomes in petitions for clemency."[13] Rather than using the mechanics of ritual to try to coerce God into mercy, the king acknowledges that any mercy received would be free and undeserved.[14]

This makes sense, especially in light of the earlier response of the sailors (Jon. 1:16). In both cases, gentiles seem to recognize the presence of a God above and beyond the web of known deities and powers—and therefore beyond manipulation. They're not taught the doctrine of God's freedom in a classroom; they're taught it by the terror of encountering the true God. It's an entailment, it seems, of the fear of the Lord they experience.

---

[13] Youngblood, *Jonah*, 139.
[14] Youngblood, *Jonah*, 140.

Nonetheless, the ignorance of Assyrians seems evident as they repent. Is "who knows?" more an affirmation of God's freedom or a confession of bewilderment? The actions of the Ninevites and the words of their king suggest they recognize a God of supreme power and righteousness. But do they know anything else about his character or ways? Do they know what they can expect of him? God is free, but that's not his only attribute. When we compare these gentiles—who until hours earlier knew only a world of idols—to the patriarchs and prophets in Jonah's lineage, we see striking differences in the way God is made known.

"I Am the God of Your Father"

In response to Jonah's message, the king of Nineveh says that the city's repentance "may" lead God to turn from his anger and, therefore, they "may not perish" (Jon. 3:9).

But when God comes to Abraham, all he does is make promises (Gen. 12:3). Abraham was a gentile and idolator. But God doesn't threaten him with judgment. He doesn't tell Abraham to repent.

When God comes to Moses, it's in response to his people's suffering in Egypt and because he "remembered his covenant with Abraham, Isaac, and Jacob" (Exod. 2:23–25). He then appears to Moses in the burning bush. He calls Moses by name and then introduces himself this way: "I am the God of your father, the God of Abraham, the God of Isaac, and the God of Jacob" (Exod. 3:4–6). He then tells Moses he's going to save his people (Exod. 3:7–8). But God doesn't threaten judgment. He doesn't tell Moses or the people to repent.

He just announces his coming grace.

God comes to Abraham and Moses as a God who makes and keeps promises. A God who has compassion on his people. A God who in his holiness is nonetheless personal, who has an indissoluble relationship with the objects of his mercy. A God of covenant—*hesed*—love.

From what we know of Jonah, the message we see him speak, and the response of Nineveh, we may doubt that the gentiles knew they were dealing with this God. God is free, but he isn't fickle or arbitrary. He desires that people repent and live (Ezek. 32).

Like the sailors, the Ninevites have a Hebrew prophet among them who knows all this. But he isn't very talkative.

The God of Promises

God is just, and he will execute justice when Jesus returns. He calls sinners to repent.

But our faith rests on the promises of God. Regarding Abraham, Paul writes:

No unbelief made him waver concerning the promise of God, but he grew strong in his faith as he gave glory to God, fully convinced that God was able to do what he had promised. That is why his faith was 'counted to him as righteousness.' But the words 'it was counted to him' were not written for his sake alone, but for ours also. It will be counted to us who believe in him who raised from the dead Jesus our Lord, who was delivered for our trespasses and raised for our justification. (Rom. 4:20–25)

The repentance of Nineveh is stunning. But did the great city know the God of promises? Did they have faith in him?

Abraham trusted in the God of covenant love. Our repentance as Christians responds to this same God. He has come to us. He has died for us. He is risen. Our righteousness—our ability to stand on the day of judgment—comes through faith in the God who so desired that sinners live that he freely went to his death for them.

Questions for Reflection

1.   What do you think it's reasonable to believe the king of Nineveh knows about God?

2.   What's the relationship between repentance and faith?

Read Jonah 3:10; Jeremiah 18:7–8

Does God Change His Plans?

All four of the uses of the Hebrew word for *repent* in the book of Jonah occur in Jonah 3:8–10.[15] Two of those refer to Nineveh, and two refer to God. It's translated as "turn." Here, in verse 10, God sees that Nineveh "turned from their evil way." As a result, "God relented of the disaster that he had said he would do to them."

Jonah, in some sense, repented in the fish. Then Nineveh repented. What does it mean, though, to say that God "turned"? He didn't have sin to repent of. Does it mean he changed his mind? Is that even possible?

God Is Merciful

It may seem like this is the climax of the story. God's call to Jonah to bring his message to Nineveh sets the dominoes falling in Jonah 1:1–3 and then, a second time, in Jonah 3:1–13. The question has been what would happen when the message finally arrived. As we see Nineveh's response, and then God's response to Nineveh, that question is answered.

---

[15] Estelle, *Salvation through Judgment and Mercy*, 113.

And we see the heart of God.

God doesn't change his mind when Nineveh repents. From our human perspective, we can speak in this way. But the God who pulled the strings of the wind and sea to bring Jonah back to him doesn't get caught by surprise. God controls everything. He knows everything. And he works through his chosen means to bring to pass what pleases him.

By reading the Ninevites' repentance in light of Jonah's sea voyage, we recognize that God has arranged everything according to his will. Nineveh's repentance has been his desire and plan from the beginning. Jonah's message offered no explicit knowledge of God's mercy or call to repentance, but the 40 days' delay implied that repentance and mercy were possible. God's word did its work, and God relents as he'd always planned to.

God's "repentance" mirrors Nineveh's because they're connected: "God is responsive to human repentance because of his mercy."[16] But it's a response he has planned from the beginning.

But Is God Just?

Jonah, though, likely has a different theological concern. It's not God's immutability—his unchanging perfection—that he cares about. It's God's justice. How can God "turn" from his wrath and still be just? As one commentator writes, "If divine mercy can so easily cancel out divine justice, then life is arbitrary and capricious."[17]

It's a profound concern. And if it is, in fact, what has driven Jonah's actions—even, possibly, his preaching of judgment in Nineveh—it's one we may be sympathetic to. It may be hard to believe that someone who has been through the ordeal he endured and then received mercy might still feel this way. But if we look in our hearts, we'll likely find similar contradictions. We demand justice. We need to know we live in a universe with a moral order. But we know we need mercy just as desperately.

The problem—which may be Jonah's problem—is that we come to elevate our own sense of justice above God's. If enough seems awry to us, we make ourselves the judge of God—even as we depend on his mercy every moment.

The King in Ashes

Why does God relent from the judgment against you? Because like the king of Nineveh, our king, Jesus, arose from his throne, took off the splendor of his royal robe, took upon himself something much lower than sackcloth—human flesh. He came down to the dust of death. He sat in ashes.

But Jesus didn't accept this humiliation because he had sinned. No sword hung over his head. No judgment threatened him. He emptied himself of his infinite royal splendor because the judgment threatened you and me. When you're in Christ, when you turn your eyes to Jesus, the judgment that threatened you is removed. God relents—eternally.

It's only through the cross that we have peace with God. And it's only through the cross that our inner contradictions find resolution. God is utterly just and infinitely merciful. He executes justice on the cross so that the guilty who look to Christ can find grace.

---

[16] Youngblood, *Jonah*, 141.

[17] Ackerman, "Jonah," 240.

By turning from our sin to Jesus, our longing for both justice and mercy is satisfied.

And when God looks down on his church and sees those who have been baptized, who have put on Christ, who have been crucified with him, he relents.

Questions for Reflection

1. What do you think it means that God repents in this scene?

2. Does God relax the perfect standards of his justice in order to have mercy on sinners?

Notes

"THAT IS WHY I MADE HASTE TO FLEE

TO TARSHISH; FOR I KNEW THAT YOU

ARE A GRACIOUS GOD AND MERCIFUL."

_____

Jonah 4:2

"Please Take My Life *from* Me"

Read Jonah 4:1; Matthew 5:21–22

The Angry Prophet

In an article titled "When Good Things Happen to Other People: How to Handle Jealousy," Emma Straub describes her reaction to the success of others as she struggled to establish her writing career:

> Every morning brought news of yet another 20-something woman with a book deal, sometimes for half a million dollars. I could have used half a million dollars! Were those women as good as I was at looking for pretend real estate on the internet? Were they as funny, as charming, as self-deprecating? They were not! Of course, I had no idea what these women were actually like. All I knew was that I hated them.
>
> Thus began my years of torment . . .. I was angry and jealous because good things were happening to other people. I was sure that I was smarter, prettier, more deserving. I was a harder worker, more prepared for wild success, more television-ready! I wanted to drown the people I knew who had sold their books—I wanted to torture them, slowly. And if once they were published those books actually sold well, I was inconsolable.
>
> It's an ugly way to feel—unhappy because of someone else's success—but human beings are often ugly. And I'm willing to bet that you've felt the same way.[1]

Is she right? Would she win that bet? What do you do when good things happen in other people's lives but not in yours?

We aren't immune to the type of ugliness Emma Straub's article describes. Neither are prophets.

What's in Jonah's Heart?

Throughout the book of Jonah, we've tried to understand Jonah's response to God's call by looking closely at his actions—what he does and what he doesn't do. When he flees God, sleeps during the storm, and tells the sailors to throw him overboard, we've looked for clues to figure out what motivates him. Even when he prays in chapter 2, we had to look at the context and the things *left out* of his prayer in order to figure out his state of mind.

Only now does the author tell us directly what Jonah feels: "But it displeased Jonah exceedingly, and he was angry" (Jon. 4:1).

What provoked Jonah's anger? God's mercy. Jonah brought his message of doom to Nineveh, but instead of watching the city burn, he sees an entire metropolis in sackcloth and ashes. The gentiles call out to God and turn from their evil ways. And God relents.

God's anger vanishes; so Jonah's erupts.

---

[1] Emma Straub, "When Good Things Happen to Other People: How to Handle Jealousy," *The Huffington Post*, April 26, 2013, https://www.huffpost.com/entry/when-good-things-happen-t_0_n_3163021.

The Bitter Irony

Jonah isn't upset because he's not getting something that other people received. He's upset because God is giving to other people what he gave to Jonah in chapter 2. God saved Jonah from death. Now God saves the Ninevites from death.

How mad is Jonah about this? "But it displeased Jonah exceedingly" (Jon. 4:1). This is a more literal translation of the Hebrew: "It was evil to Jonah—great evil." It's the same word used in Jonah 3:10, which says that Nineveh "turned from their evil way." It's also used in Jonah 1:2, when God called Jonah and said, "call out against it, for their evil has come up before me."

But there's something unique in this verse. To Jonah, what God did was "exceedingly" evil. According to Jonah, what's even worse than the sin of the Ninevites? The fact that God forgave them.

Jonah's bitterness at God's love brings us to the tragically ironic heart of this story.

"Crucify Him"

Religion doesn't save us from envy and resentment. In the story of Jonah, we have a man who's supposed to be spiritual—a prophet called by God. If he isn't immune, then neither are we.

The author of Jonah wants us to see Jonah's sin. But he doesn't want us to wag our fingers at Jonah self-righteously. Instead, he wants us to see the resentment in our own hearts, and repent.

When Jesus died, God's anger against us relented. But it was the anger of religious men that put him on the cross. After Jesus's arrest, Pontius Pilate offered to release him:

> "Do you want me to release for you the King of the Jews?" For he perceived that it was out of envy that the chief priests had delivered him up. But the chief priests stirred up the crowd to have him release to them Barabbas instead. And Pilate again said to them, "Then what shall I do with the man you call the King of the Jews?" And they cried out again, "Crucify him." And Pilate said to them, "Why? What evil has he done?" But they shouted all the more, "Crucify him." (Mark 15:9–14)

Those who knew the Scriptures inside-out—the Bible-believers—should have been the first to worship Israel's Messiah. They should have led the people to their king. They should have rejoiced more than anyone in God's forgiveness. Instead, driven by envy, they incite the crowd to murder.

Jesus threatened everything they *actually* treasured: their security, status, and authority. So their anger erupted.

Questions for Reflection

1. Are you tempted to feel like you're entitled to certain things because you're a Christian? If so, what? God promised us things, and he'll keep his promises, but often we add our own expectations to what God has said.

2. Has there ever been anyone you hoped wouldn't repent and find peace with God?

Read Jonah 4:2; Exodus 32:1–10; Jonah 2:7–9

The Known God

Jonah, "exceedingly" angry because God spared Nineveh, decides to pray. He prayed in the fish's belly, and now he prays for a second time in this story. And as ugly as Jonah's anger may seem to us, he's not fleeing to the end of the earth like he did in chapter 1. He stays in God's presence—and lashes out.

As we'll see, this is the first time God and Jonah respond to each other. When God called Jonah in chapters 1 and 3, Jonah said nothing. When Jonah called out to God from the fish, God said nothing. He just told the fish to spit him out. Now, in chapter 4, they have a conversation.

Who Does Jonah Pray To?

Who does Jonah pray to here? That may seem obvious. But the answer helps us understand Jonah's anger.

Throughout the book of Jonah, God is called "the Lord" when he interacts with Jonah (Jon. 1:1; 2:1, 10; 3:1). He is also called "the Lord" when the sailors pray to him (Jon. 1:14). That's one reason to think they're truly converted: "the Lord" (*Yahweh*) is God's covenant name. It's the name that those who know and belong to him call him.

With the Ninevites, though, he is "God" (*elohim*). They recognize him as the supreme power, the creator and judge, but not, it seems, as the covenant God of Abraham, Isaac, and Jacob—the God of promises.

So Jonah, who thinks God has done a great evil, still addresses God as the Lord he knows: "O Lord."

In fact, his covenant knowledge of God is the basis of his complaint. He says, "O Lord, is not this what I said when I was yet in my country? That is why I made haste to flee to Tarshish; for I knew that you are a gracious God and merciful, slow to anger and abounding in steadfast love, and relenting from disaster" (Jon. 4:2). It's *because* he knows God that he is angry.

He knows God's character. He has received God's promises and covenant love. He knows what God is like. That's why he's angry.

And now he says this intimate knowledge of God has motivated him from the very beginning of the story. Why did Jonah disobey God? Why did he make "haste to flee to Tarshish"?

Because, unlike the sailors and the Assyrians, he *knew* God.

Could there be a more absurd irony? How does that make any sense?

Abounding in *Hesed* Love

How does Jonah know God is gracious? Jonah quotes Exodus 34:6–8, which reports God's words to Moses shortly after the Israelites worshiped the golden calf (Exod. 32). At first, God responded to Israel's idolatry with anger (Exod. 32:9–10). He told Moses he'd judge Israel for their betrayal. The ink was barely dry, so to speak, on the two stone tablets that established his covenant with his people (Exod. 31:18) and already they'd committed spiritual adultery.

But then Moses cried out on behalf of Israel, and God said, about himself, "The Lord, the Lord, a God merciful and gracious, slow to anger, and abounding in steadfast love and faithfulness, forgiving iniquity and transgression and sin" (Exod. 34:6–7). So, God tells Moses to make new tablets, and he renews his covenant with his people (Exod. 34).

Jonah tells God that he remembers God's mercy to Israel.

And, in this story, Jonah experienced it personally. In the fish, he prayed, "I trust in your steadfast love" (Jon. 2:8). Jonah had hope because he knew God's covenant love. He knew God was gracious, merciful, slow to anger, and relenting from disaster. That's the reason he knew God would save him.

But it's also the reason he ran from God in the beginning. And it's the reason he's furious now. God's love makes Jonah exceedingly angry.

God's *hesed* love is the hinge of the book of Jonah. It drives all the main character's actions—for good and for evil.

Nineveh at the Judgment

The author hasn't shown us the wickedness of the pagans in this story. He shows both the sailors and the Ninevites in a sympathetic light. They're in trouble and come across as humble and desperate for help. We feel for them. And when they turn to God, we feel relief.

But Jonah, God's prophet, seems only to get uglier. He's God's covenant lawyer, who's been in the divine council and anointed by the Holy Spirit. But he's even less sympathetic now than at first.

And it's God's covenant people that Jesus, hundreds of years later, compares to pagan Nineveh: "This generation is an evil generation. It seeks for a sign, but no sign will be given to it except the sign of Jonah. For as Jonah became a sign to the people of Nineveh, so will the Son of Man be to this generation" (Luke 11:29). Jesus comes to Israel, he says, like Jonah went to Nineveh. His resurrection will be a sign of his divine commission, as Jonah's return from the fish was a sign.

But Jesus doesn't just put God's people in the place of the Ninevites. He says the Ninevites, unlike Israel in Jesus's day, responded to God's word: "The men of Nineveh will rise up at the judgment with this generation and condemn it, for they repented at the preaching of Jonah, and behold, something greater than Jonah is here" (Luke 11:32).

Jesus compares his mission to Jonah's. Yet it's Jonah who, like many in Jesus's time, refuses to truly repent. As a true prophet, called by God and speaking God's word, Jonah is like Jesus. As a sinful member of God's covenant people, calling God's work of salvation evil and lashing out, Jonah is like many of the Jews in Jesus's generation.

Questions for Reflection

1. What are the two names of God in Jonah? What does each mean?

2. Do you think the pagans in this book—the sailors and the Ninevites—are sympathetic characters? If so, why do you think the author portrays them this way?

Read Jonah 1:12, 4:3–4; Proverbs 17:15

The Death Wish

Jonah is exceedingly angry. He's angry because God relented from anger. He's enraged that God has not destroyed Nineveh.

Now, Jonah quantifies this great anger in concrete terms: "Therefore now, O Lord, please take my life from me, for it is better for me to die than to live" (Jon. 4:3). How angry is Jonah? So angry that his own life has no value to him. So angry that death becomes more desirable than life.

And then God responds to him for the first time: "Do you do well to be angry?" (Jon. 4:4).

We shouldn't dismiss this question. It's a serious one. We may see Jonah as ridiculous. It seems absurd that he'd be angry about God's mercy and love, especially after he's received it himself. It's the only reason he's still alive.

But Jonah isn't this angry just because good things are happening to *other* people—it's because good things are happening to *bad* people. The great question in the book of Job, at least as it's commonly stated, is "Why do bad things happen to good people?" Jonah's question is "Why do good things happen to bad people?"[2]

Should people who flay their enemies and hang the skins on their city walls go unpunished? Should people who crush their neighbors and gloat about their power be allowed to evade justice? God's mercy can, in fact, be deeply troubling. As we've noted earlier, it raises a profound question about God's justice.

Now God asks it himself. Is Jonah right to be angry?

Hurl Me into the Sea

The question, *Does Jonah want to die?* came up earlier in this story.

In chapter 1, from the moment Jonah refuses his calling, he begins moving down—down to Joppa, down into the ship, then down into the inner part of the ship, and finally into the sea. Jonah descends throughout the first scene until he is in "the belly of *Sheol*" (Jon. 2:2). He doesn't literally die—God saves him at the last moment—but he comes as close to death as he could. And from the moment he defied God, a death sentence hung over him. He was a dead man walking.

Jonah knew this, because he knew God. Yet his motives weren't entirely clear. Did he, even from the moment of God's call, *want* to die? Or was he just resigned to death as an inevitable consequence of his actions? He knew God was gracious, as he now says explicitly in Jonah 4:2. He could have called out to God for mercy at any time.

But he let the storm rage. He let the sailors come to brink of death. He let himself be thrown overboard. He preferred to endure all these things rather than pray to God.

Jonah's instructions to the sailors, "Pick me up and hurl me into the sea" (Jon. 1:12), super-ficially resembled an act of self-sacrifice. Jonah now, though, seems to confirm our doubts about this: "it is better for me to die than to live" (Jon. 4:8). If you place no value on your life, offering it up is no sacrifice. At the last moment in the fish, he may have discovered a desire to live, but his statement now seems to fit with his trajectory throughout the book of Jonah.

Jonah isn't the first person in the Bible to long for God's vengeance. He isn't the first to wonder why it's delayed:

> O Lord, God of vengeance,
> O God of vengeance, shine forth!
> Rise up, O judge of the earth;
> repay the proud what they deserve!
> O Lord, how long shall the wicked,
> how long shall the wicked exult? (Ps. 94:1–3)

He also isn't the first to see the injustice in the world and prefer death to life. The preacher of

---

[2] Ackerman, "Jonah," 240.

Ecclesiastes writes:

> Again I saw all the oppressions that are done under the sun. And behold, the tears of the oppressed, and they had no one to comfort them! On the side of their oppressors there was power, and there was no one to comfort them. And I thought the dead who are already dead more fortunate than the living who are still alive. But better than both is he who has not yet been and has not seen the evil deeds that are done under the sun. (Eccl. 4:1–3)

If the wicked remain free to rampage, it's only a matter of time before Israel will be overthrown. Doesn't God's mercy to Nineveh makes his covenant promises to Israel worthless?[3]

The Death of Infinite Value

We all need an answer to this question if life is going to be worth living. If others can rape and slaughter with impunity, our lives have no ultimate worth. We need to know God's mercy doesn't cancel out his justice.

But we need mercy just as much as those who sin against us. This, ultimately, is unacceptable to Jonah. If we call on God to be just, we're asking him to call us to account for our own acts of injustice. We need, somehow, God's justice and mercy to exist together, without one diminishing the other.

We need the cross.

On the cross, God's justice is done and his covenant promises are kept. The sacrifices in the Old Testament law pointed Israel to the future, when God would reconcile his mercy and his justice.

They're the blood sacrifices Jonah seems unwilling to make.

Questions for Reflection

1. Do you sympathize at all with Jonah? Why or why not?

2. Has the injustice and oppression in the world ever seemed unbearable to you? If so, how has God helped you find hope? How does God reconcile his mercy and justice?

---

[3] Youngblood, *Jonah*, 160

Notes

"AND SHOULD NOT I PITY NINEVEH,

THAT GREAT CITY?"

Jonah 4:11

The God *of* Compassion

Read Jonah 4:5–6; Genesis 13:11–13; Numbers 14:26–30

Jonah's Joy

God asks Jonah a question: "Do you do well to be angry?" (Jon. 4:4). He asks this question again in Jonah 4:9. This is the only question God asks in the book of Jonah. Given that it also comes at the conclusion, as Jonah's heart is revealed, we should probably see it as central to the book and its message.

What will Jonah's answer be? What will Jonah, this man who has refused to repent and who'd rather die than live, say when asked by God about the justice of his actions?

Nothing. He doesn't answer God.

Like when God called him in Jonah 1:1–2 and 3:1–2, Jonah leaves God's presence without responding.[1] Again, the author indicates that Jonah, despite his second chance, hasn't changed.

Instead, he goes to find a comfortable place to sit and watch what happens to Nineveh. Even now, it seems, he holds out hope that God will destroy the great city. It may be that he saw his accusation as a test for God. Will God now relent from his mercy and prove himself just?

As Jonah waits to find out, God provides a plant to give him shade from the desert sun. And Jonah's anger turns to joy.

East of Nineveh

Instead of going west toward Tarshish, Jonah now goes east of the city: "Jonah went out of the city and sat to the east of the city" (Jon. 4:5). First, he moved in the direction opposite of God's command (Jon. 1:3). Then, he went to Nineveh in obedience to God (Jon. 3:3). This seems to show Jonah's repentance, his "turning" from his own will to God's will. But what does this eastward movement out of the city mean? The author didn't need to tell us the direction, so the inclusion of this detail means something.

In the Old Testament, especially in the foundational stories in Genesis that reveal God's relationship with humanity, east means exile: separation from God. He sends Adam and Eve out of Eden to the east (Gen. 3:24). Cain settles east of Eden after leaving God's presence (Gen. 4:16). When Lot leaves Abraham, he goes east to live in Sodom and Gomorrah (Gen. 13:11).[2] East means separation from God's presence. Nineveh was the land east of Israel. Now Jonah is east of Nineveh.

Although Jonah has judged God for his mercy, it is Jonah who now goes in the direction of exile, under the shadow of God's coming judgment. Jonah finds a place to sit to watch the destruction he hopes to see, but it's his own condition that becomes the focus. He began the story in God's presence (Jon. 1:1–2). He was later restored to God's presence (Jon. 3:1–2). And he's still in God's presence.

---

[1] Youngblood, *Jonah*, 165.
[2] Youngblood, *Jonah*, 165.

But he's moving in the wrong direction again.

Gimme Shelter

East of Nineveh, Jonah sets up a hut for himself. He "made a booth for himself there. He sat under it in the shade, till he should see what would become of the city" (Jon. 4:5). Jonah, rejecting God's will, has again placed himself in a dangerous natural environment.

But then God gives another, better shelter to "save him": "Now the Lord God appointed a plant and made it come up over Jonah, that it might be a shade over his head, to save him from his discomfort" (Jon. 3:6). God "appointed" the fish that sheltered Jonah in the sea (Jon. 1:17), and now he appoints the plant. He continues to show mercy to Jonah. He continues to shelter him from nature—and the wrath that great waters and the desert reveal (Gen. 7:17–23; Num. 14:26–30).

And he continues to show his sovereign power over all creatures.

Jonah loves the plant. Rather than being "exceedingly" angry, he's "exceedingly glad because of the plant" (Jon. 3:7). The comfort and security bring him joy.

We know what makes him mad. Now we know what brings him delight—his own comfort and safety. He delights in God's special provision for *him*. Jonah, like Israel, loves the privilege of being chosen by God, but not the call to bring the blessings he's received from God to others.

What about us? What do we delight in? We may praise God when the doctor says our cancer is benign. We may rejoice in him when we have plenty of savings in the bank. We may say he's faithful when our kids get into good colleges and have a smooth road ahead of them in life.

We may thank him for saving us from our sin.

But what about our neighbor, who cursed at us when we parked in his spot? The awkward woman at church who's so draining to talk to? The drunk driver who crippled our son?

Is it our delight to love these people? Is it our delight to bring them good news?

What Shelter Do We Need?

Our natural instinct, as sinners, is to set up booths for ourselves—comfortable places to sit, protected from pain and loss. We make booths out of things like money, good health, career accomplishments, romantic relationships, and political power. These things aren't necessarily bad, but they don't offer the shelter we think they do. They can disappear in a moment.

And none of them shelters us from death. None of them protects us from the wrath of God.

But God has provided us shelter. He provided another tree. It gives us eternal refuge:

> These are the ones coming out of the great tribulation. They have washed their robes
> and made them white in the blood of the Lamb.
> Therefore they are before the throne of God,
> and serve him day and night in his temple;
> and he who sits on the throne will shelter them with his presence.
> They shall hunger no more; neither thirst anymore;
> the sun shall not strike them,

nor any scorching heat.
For the Lamb in the midst of the throne will be their shepherd,
and he will guide them to springs of living water,
and God will wipe away every tear from their eyes. (Rev. 7:15–17)

We're all born east of Eden. We're exiles, waiting for the judgment. We bear our father Adam's curse.

But the second Adam is the Lamb. His blood makes us pure and spotless, so his throne becomes our shelter. In the tree he provides, his cross, the tension between God's justice and mercy is resolved in history. And eternally.

Questions for Reflection

1. What is significant about Jonah setting up camp east of Nineveh? Why do you think the author bothered to mention the direction?

2. Why does Jonah love the plant? What might his great joy in the plant reveal about his character?

Read Jonah 4:7–9; 2 Kings 17:1–23

Angry Enough to Die

Jonah's fury at God's mercy suggests that he thinks God misgoverns the universe and has compromised his covenant with Israel. Youngblood writes, "The book of Jonah focuses on two questions that preoccupied all of the prophets: (1) How do divine mercy and divine justice interact without canceling each other out? (2) How do God's sovereignty and his particular covenant with Israel interact without canceling each other out?"[3]

God uses the plant as an "object lesson" to offer his answer. He takes away the shelter the plant provided and repeats his earlier question, now specifically referring to the plant: "Do you do well to be angry for the plant?" (Jon. 4:9).

---

[3] Youngblood, *Jonah*, 28–29.

Jonah's answer echoes his earlier statement: "Yes, I do well to be angry, angry enough to die" (Jon. 4:9). For the first time, he answers God. And these are his final words in the book.

The Plant's Death

Jonah went from "exceedingly" angry (Jon. 4:1) to "exceedingly glad" (Jon. 4:6). Now, God assaults him: "But when dawn came up the next day, God appointed a worm that attacked the plant, so that it withered. When the sun rose, God appointed a scorching east wind, and the sun beat down on the head of Jonah so that he was faint" (Jon. 4:7).

God appoints three things here in chapter 4. He appoints the plant that grows up over Jonah and provides shade. This is a desert climate that can be scorching. Shade is a precious commodity.

Then he appoints a worm that attacks the plant, which withers and dies. Jonah loses his shade.

Then, God appoints a scorching east wind to torment Jonah until he's ready to pass out. This would likely be an east wind coming down from the mountains of Iran that reach 60 miles per hour. These hot, dry, dusty winds—like the Santa Ana winds in California—blow on him furiously. The rays of the sun bake him.

The God of the sea and dry land controls everything. He gives and withholds grace as he wills.

Jonah, like the plant, begins to wither.

Who Shelters Jonah?

Jonah has set up camp east of Nineveh—the direction of exile. He has lashed out at God. He's appointed himself as God's judge. He seems to be moving away from God's presence.

But God continues to sustain him. In fact, he responds to Jonah's accusations even though Jonah deserves the death he has requested. Something has changed, though. Until now, God has been called "the Lord" in reference to his relationship with Jonah. Now he is "the Lord God" (*Yahweh-Elohim*). One commentator says:

> In 4:6 the sudden use of the compound divine name, Yahweh-Elohim, catches the attention of the reader and signals a temporary and meaningful switch. The object lesson then uses Elohim through its conclusion in 4:9. This suggests that Jonah has been relocated among the non-Israelites in the object lesson.[4]

God doesn't change. But this name change suggests that his relationship with Jonah isn't the same. And Jonah, as we've said, likely represents Israel.

Israel broke its covenant with God all the way back in the days of Solomon. Shortly after building the temple—the house of the Lord—in Jerusalem, Solomon introduced idol worship into Israel. He brought the gods of the nations into the land—and hearts—of God's holy people (1 Kings 11:4–13). As a result, God divided Israel, taking most of the tribes away from Solomon's line (1 Kings 11:29–36).

Yet, just as he relented from destroying the Israelites after they worshiped the golden calf, he allowed generation after generation to pass without executing the judgment he had promised in

---

[4] Walton, "Jonah," 270.

the law. He said that if Israel disobeyed, they—like Adam and Eve before them—would be sent away from God's presence (Deut. 28:36). He has relented. He has held back his wrath.

But he won't forever. Exile lies ahead. Not long after Jonah, the Assyrians will conquer the Northern Kingdom—where Jonah lived—and capture the people (2 Kings 17:1–23). They'll be taken from the promised land and never return.

Is Jonah Right to Be Angry?

As Jonah withers in the desert winds, God asks Jonah, "Do you do well to be angry about the plant?" (Jon. 4:9).

Now, Jonah answers God: "Yes, I do well to be angry, angry enough to die" (Jon. 4:9). He doubles down even though he may now be in real physical danger. He means it. His anger is so great that he prefers death to life.

Jonah, at last, has given his answer: he is right to be angry about the plant.

But he doesn't get the last word.

Questions for Reflection

1. What's significant about God's name in this section?

2. What do you think is going to happen to Jonah?

Read Jonah 4:10–11; Job 42:1–6; Matthew 12:38–42

God's Pity vs. Jonah's Pity

The book of Jonah ends with God explaining his object lesson to Jonah. God compares the plant, which Jonah pities, to Nineveh, which God pities. Jonah loved the plant because it gave him comfort and protection. But God says, "And should I not pity Nineveh, that great city?" (Jon. 4:11).

The author has prepared us for this ending. He has portrayed both the sailors and the Ninevites sympathetically. We're ready to affirm and celebrate God's pity. He's the God of compassion.

But the author doesn't show us Jonah's response. It's likely, then, that he also wants to confront his readers with this object lesson. It's for them. The human author had his fellow Jews in mind. The Holy Spirit, who inspired the Scripture, had us in mind, too.

What Does God Pity?

God makes two points about the plant. First, God gave it to Jonah. Second, it didn't last. "You pity the plant, for which you did not labor, nor did you make it grow, which came into being in a night and perished in a night" (Jon. 4:10). Jonah only has the plant because God gave it to him. And God just as easily takes it away. In fact, that's what Jonah wanted God to do to Nineveh: remove his mercy.[5]

Then God says, "And should I not pity Nineveh, that great city, in which there are more than 120,000 persons who do not know their right hand from their left, and also much cattle?" (Jon. 4:11). If Jonah is upset when God removes a small mercy from him, shouldn't God care even more about a great city of so many people (and cattle!)? They're wicked (Jon. 1:2), but God now emphasizes their ignorance. That's what the idiom "do not know their right hand from their left" means. They don't know God like Jonah does.

So, is Jonah right to be angry? God has given his answer to the question. No, Jonah isn't right to be angry. We don't know what Jonah thought about this. The book of Jonah ends with God and Jonah offering opposing answers. We don't see, as we do at the end of Job, a reconciliation between God and the man who questioned God's justice (Job 42:1–6).

God is compassionate. But Jonah—and Israel—don't reflect that compassion. They were called to follow God's law and reflect his character, but they've often failed. Jonah wouldn't have been upset if God killed all 120,000 Ninevites. He would've been happy about it. But he's mad when God kills his plant. He cares more about his own comfort than other people's souls.

What Do You Pity?

Can you identify with Jonah yet? You'd probably say that you want God's mercy to reach the world. You want people to know the God of compassion. You want people to experience his grace.

---

[5] Youngblood, *Jonah*, 173.

But do you care more about your own comfort? How often do we avoid talking about the gospel because it makes us uncomfortable? How often is the primary factor in our decisions—where to live, how we spend our money, who we spend time with—our comfort?

Sometimes, as Christians, we live convoluted, incoherent lives. We get mad when good things happen to other people. We pray, think, and worry more about "the plant" than the people around us. We spend all our time on our security and comfort instead of thinking about eternal souls. That's the ugly truth.

Do you value eternal souls over your own comfort?

God does. Christ came to endure anguish of body and soul to save people like us, who at times say, "I'm angry enough to die."

Jonah thinks he is more deserving of good things than the people of Nineveh. Have you lost sight of God's mercy toward you? Have you forgotten his incomprehensible love for you? Have you lost sight of Jesus Christ's sacrifice of himself for you?

Jesus delights to bring his mercy to sinners. May we, if we've received this mercy, be willing to lay down our lives for others.

The Last Word

The book of Jonah isn't mainly about Jonah, or Nineveh, or us. It's about God. The book begins with an announcement of God's coming justice. But now, at the end, as the last word, we see the main point. He's the God of compassion. He's a God who has compassion on even the most evil human beings. This final note in Jonah resonates profoundly with us when we see the depths of evil in our souls. Hope seeps into our darkness.

Jonah knew this about God. He recognized it right away. Mercy was hidden within the message of doom God called him to deliver.

So, God's compassion is the last word. But, in this case, is the last word really the last word? God's object lesson reveals Jonah's twisted thinking. But does it answer what may be the book's main question: how does God's compassion—his *hesed* love—fit with his justice?

Maybe, in Jonah, the last word is actually in the middle. Maybe the object lesson should lead us back to the sign of Jonah. God is compassionate, but how can he also be just? The sign of Jonah tells us what Jonah himself refused to see.

When Jonah offered to be thrown overboard, it looked superficially like an act of self-sacrifice. But a sacrifice of blood never appears in the book of Jonah. No sacrifice that atones for sin occurs. The sacrifice that could enable God to be both perfectly just and infinitely merciful remained in the future. But the sign of Jonah points to it.

"For just as Jonah was three days and three nights in the belly of the great fish, so will the Son of Man be three days and three nights in the heart of the earth" (Matt. 12:40).

The one "greater than Jonah" has come (Matt. 12:41). He is risen.

Questions for Reflection

1. How willing do you think you are to bear discomfort or pain—to sacrifice yourself—for the sake of the gospel?

2. What are some gifts of God's grace that you're taking for granted right now? Where does your heart lack gratitude to God?

Notes

Resources

Core Radio Episode 103, "Understanding the Sign of Jonah." https://corechristianity.com/resource-library/episodes/understanding-the-sign-of-jonah/

Downs, Richard. "Jonah and the Whale," *Modern Reformation*, September 1, 2010. https://modernreformation.org/resource-library/articles/jonah-and-the-whale/

Estelle, Bryan D. *Salvation through Judgment and Mercy: The Gospel According to Jonah*. P&R Publishing: Phillipsburg, NJ, 2005.

Pauling, Joshua. "'He Came Down From Heaven': Divine Descent amidst a Culture of Ascent," *Modern Reformation*, December 16, 2020. https://modernreformation.org/resource-library/web-exclusive-articles/he-came-down-from-heaven-divine-descent-amidst-a-culture-of-ascent/

Timmer, Daniel C. *A Gracious and Compassionate God: Mission, Salvation, and Spirituality in the Book of Jonah*. Downers Grove, IL: InterVarsity Press, 2011.

Youngblood, Kevin J. *Jonah*, Zondervan Exegetical Commentary on the Old Testament, vol. 28, ed. Daniel I. Block. Grand Rapids, MI: Zondervan, 2013.

Made in the USA
Columbia, SC
07 August 2024

39748839R00067